# How to Write a Movie in 21 Days

## THE INNER MOVIE METHOD

# Viki King

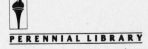

PERENNIAL LIBRARY

HARPER & ROW, PUBLISHERS, NEW YORK
CAMBRIDGE, PHILADELPHIA, SAN FRANCISCO, WASHINGTON
LONDON, MEXICO CITY, SÃO PAULO, SINGAPORE, SYDNEY

FIRST EDITION

Designer: Barbara DuPree Knowles

Copy editor: David Sassian

Indexer: Meryl Schneider for Riofrancos and Co.

Library of Congress Cataloging-in-Publication Data
King, Viki.
    How to write a movie in 21 days.
    Includes index.
    1. Moving-picture plays—Technique.   I.  Title.
PN1996.K48   1988      808'.066791    87-45632
ISBN 0-06-055112-7
ISBN 0-06-096240-2 (pbk.)

88  89  90  91  92  FG  10  9  8  7  6  5  4  3  2  1
88  89  90  91  92  FG  10  9  8  7  6  5  4  3  2  1

# PRAISE FOR VIKI KING

"Viki King manages to demystify the art and science of screenwriting. Speaking from the heart and later, spotlighting concepts from the head, Viki King presents tactics that place writing in the unstressed context of nonthreatening time management. The idea of eight, nine, and ten minute sessions is wonderfully simple, promisingly adaptive, and joyfully do-able."

*—Dr. Maisha Hazzard,*
PROFESSOR OF COMMUNICATIONS
OHIO UNIVERSITY

"I admit it—my perfectionism is an obstacle. I procrastinate a lot and your 'just write it don't think about it' method was perfect for me."

*—Amy Harris*

"Thanks to Viki, I am a screenwriter. My life is now different. Old things have passed away, all things have become new. I am amazed at Viki's insight into human life, experience and need."

*—Don Cleary*

"It helps reduce the ominous task of writing a screenplay into something that can be done 8 minutes at a time. I used to think of the pre-writing phase as something that required tremendous preparation. I now realize that it's as easy as picking up a pen."

*—Dan Kendall*

# How to Write a Movie in 21 Days

# CONTENTS

# ACKNOWLEDGMENTS

Thanks to Syd Field. I recommend to you, as I do to my students, his books *Screenplay* and *The Screenwriter's Workbook.* (I tell my students he's the father of structure. They call me the mother of content.)

Thanks to Linda Venis; head of the Writer's Program at UCLA Extension. Because of her untiring passion, the UCLA Writer's Program is unsurpassed in excellence. Thanks to Mickey Loy and Darlene Blackburn and staff. They are a joy to work with.

Thanks to my students and clients. When the student is ready, the teacher appears. I think also, when the teacher is ready the students appear.

Thanks to Ron Fricano, samurai scriptwriter, whose insights first revealed that we write from our hearts; rewrite from our heads.

Thanks to Connie Clausen, my agent. She's got a sign over her desk that says, "Just Do The Damn Thing," and she does.

Thanks to Connie's associate, Guy Kettelhack, for his expert hard work and kind concern.

Thanks to Larry Ashmead, executive editor at Harper & Row, for being impeccably classy.

Thanks to Sallie Coolidge, editor, for her professional efficiency and generous cooperation.

Thanks to Micele Price, who was there for the last marathon read-through. I wish for you a Micele to help share the process.

Thanks to Leigh Chorlton for being a great friend and an equally great line editor.

Thanks to Buddy Collette for his unerring patience, rock solid values, remarkable talent, infinite wisdom. Thank you so very much for being there while I was getting there.

Thanks to Barbara Elman Schiffman, who typed this thing. She was unfailingly generous with her energies. She even got the flu so I didn't have to.

Thanks to you for daring to take a whack at your Inner Movie. I hope it gives you something of value.

From the heart,

1988

**DANIEL**
But how do I know if my picture's the
right one?

**MIYAGI**
If comes from inside you, always right
one.

from *Karate Kid* by Robert Mark Kamen

# How to Write a Movie in 21 Days

The Big
Picture

# PROMISES, PROMISES

So you want to write a movie? You've come to the right place!

The Inner Movie Method takes you the shortest distance from your great idea to a completed screenplay.

It covers everything you need to know about structure, content, and characters; it even tells you where to set the tabs on the typewriter.

The Inner Movie Method will help you find out what you want to write and then help you write it.

## How to use this book

This book is divided into three sections: *Beginning, Middle and End*, just like a screenplay. Beginning is set-up, middle is action, and end is resolution. We'll set up your movie. You'll write the movie. We'll resolve any obstacles that keep you from finishing your movie.

### BEGINNING: HOW TO GET READY.

This is where we'll work out everything you'll need to write your movie. We'll find your story, discover your characters, work out the best structure for your story, and then show you how it should look on the page.

Here's a sample of what you will get:

- *How to know what your idea is:*
  Exercises to find out what you want to say.
  Actions to get you to say it.
- *How to tell if your idea is really a movie*:
  Find out if your idea is a song, a play, or a novel, rather than a movie, and what to do if it is.
- *How to become a technical expert in 2 pages*:
  Type the 2-Page Picture Show and thereby discover all you'll need to know about screenplay form.

## MIDDLE: WRITING YOUR MOVIE IN 21 DAYS

Here's where you'll do it. You'll write a fast random draft from your heart; you'll rewrite from your head. This section shows every step you need to take and when you need to take it to complete your script.

Here are some questions you'll find answered:

- *How did I lose my hero and how do I get him back?*
- *What's my story again? I keep forgetting.*
- *How come nothing's happening?*
- *How do I get my characters to talk like real people?*
- *I know the beginning and I know the end, now how do I get here from there?*

We'll go hand in hand, step-by-step, all the way through your movie. You'll even learn:

- *How to Know When You're Done:*
  Test questions that can only be answered when the script is absolutely finished.
- *How to Pick Two People for a Test Reading* (excluding all members of your immediate household):
  Questions you ask the reader to find out if you said what you wanted to say.
  Questions to have the reader ask you to find out if you've said it the best possible way.

## END: EMBRACING THE IMPOSSIBLE OBSTACLES

This is where we'll demystify any blocks, doubts, or circumstantial difficulties you might have along the way.

No other screenwriting book deals with the fact that you think you're going to die of this. You'll use this section to identify why you've stopped, so you can take action to keep going. We'll cover:

- *How to keep going when you think you can't.*
  Statements you can have a loved one say to you.
  Confidence builders, including "How to Write a Fan Letter to Yourself."
- *Why you have to believe you can do it and what to do when you don't.*
- *Why you get the flu when you're on Page 90.*
- *Exercises to keep going. Pick one; pick ten—don't stop.*

And if it's too hard and you just can't go on, the Inner Movie Method covers such details as

- *Where to arrange your workspace.*
- *How to schedule work time.*
- *What to say to your spouse when you can't come to bed.*

Chances are you'll want to go directly to the section on how much money you're going to make. In *There's No Business Like Show Business*, you'll find answers to these questions.

- Do I need an agent?
- How do I get an agent?
- What do I do until I get an agent?

And we'll go even further.

- How do I know when I'm in the business?
- Can I succeed in Hollywood if I live in Buffalo?

The Inner Movie Method asks all the obscure questions you haven't thought of and answers all the questions you already have.

We won't say "this is the definition of this" and "that is the meaning of that." You just start right in, right away, and finish before you can worry about how to begin.

So, grab a pencil and the blank page you haven't been able to fill; we're going to write a movie. The Inner Movie.

# WHAT IS THE INNER MOVIE METHOD?

A colleague at the Writers Guild, upon hearing about *How to Write a Movie in 21 Days* said, "What are you, crazy? It's almost impossible to write a movie no matter how much time you have."

Here's a secret:

My colleague is right.

And yet there are thousands of people trying to do the impossible.

That's why the Inner Movie Method was created—to find ways to make an impossible thing possible.

Here's what the Inner Movie Method is, in one line: *Write from your heart; rewrite from your head.*

Since no one in their right mind can write a movie, let's not use the mind. Let's use the heart.

Your heart is smarter than you think it is, and it knows the movie that you want to write, so we circumvent all the doubt, the unfamiliarity with the form, and we go directly to the heart.

## How to put your head in your heart's hands

Writing is schizophrenic in that it uses two parts of you. There's the heart part, which already feels your movie, and the head part, which gets it on paper.

We humans are schizophrenic in that we must juggle our

right and left brains, our conscious and unconscious, our analytical and intuitive faculties.

Harmony in our lives comes in balancing these aspects of ourselves and knowing when to use which.

When we create, there are four distinct modes we use:

*Exploration.* Take it all in, do research, ask questions, be aware of connections, make sense out of nonsense.

*Creation.* Brainstorm, play with all the material, shake it, smell it, look at it upside down, see it in new ways from all angles through unlimited thinking.

*Decision.* Now hone and decide what way to look at it. Eliminate everything that doesn't serve your single vision.

*Action.* Put it into being. Schedule and plan and implement.

These modes will not occur linearly. One minute you need to brainstorm, the next you need to come in out of the "brainstorm" and dry your socks.

This dance between the modes occurs naturally. Your heart knows when to use which, but your head doesn't always believe this. The head believes that this mode-changing is its job, and so it interferes with the heart, tries to grab the throttle, and messes with the whole natural process.

It's a simple mix-up to solve. The Inner Movie Method keeps your mind busy with jobs that your mind can do very well.

That leaves your heart deliciously free to create a great movie.

The Inner Movie Method assigns specific jobs to your head and your heart so that each part of you is doing the job it does best and then not interfering with one another.

## What are these jobs and who's going to do them?

You'll need techniques to find out who your story is about and what the story is about.

Once you know who and what you'll need to know how you're going to write it.

You need techniques to structure your story so that you have a beginning, middle, and end.

You'll need techniques to get the story on the paper so that it looks like a movie.

You'll need exercises that continue to help you keep your horse before your cart.

You'll need a shoulder to cry on and someone to celebrate with.

Here are some of the specific jobs we give to your head:

### THE 9-MINUTE MOVIE

Before you even start writing you'll know what goes on pages 1, 3, 10, 30, 45, 60, 75, 90, and 120 of your screenplay. It's a map to get you through the Act II desert so you don't aimlessly wander off the page.

### THE 2-PAGE PICTURE SHOW

One of the major fears of first-time screenwriters is how it's supposed to look on the page. Actually, screenplay formatting is the easiest facet of the whole thing. So, we'll make you a technical whiz by typing two pages. Once you have the bones you can get on to the meat.

Here are a few heart jobs:

### THE 8-MINUTE AUTHOR

This is how we find out what's in your heart. We're not going to try and let our mind figure it out or analyze or guess.

We'll do this very simply. We're going to ask. It's a way to find out fast what's on your heart's mind. Once we circumvent your head, it's wonderfully easy to tap your wellspring of feelings. And feelings are going to write your movie.

As an 8-minute author you will experience quick breakthroughs to what you really want, what you really hope, and what you really care to say. And you're going to keep in touch with yourself all the way.

When you see this line ⁓⁓⁓⁓⁓⁓⁓⁓⁓⁓⁓⁓⁓⁓ that's your chance to write. At first these are small exercises that are designed to get your movie out 8 minutes at a time. Later it's the techniques that you will use to actually write your movie.

### HOW YOUR AGE REVEALS WHAT'S ON YOUR MIND

You'll need techniques to find who this is about and what the story is. There is a section on the specific life themes we all tend to land on at specific ages in our lives. You can look up your age and realize that the central life question that you are experiencing in your life is exactly the issue of your movie. By writing it you will answer it.

### EMBRACING THE IMPOSSIBLE OBSTACLE

You will need techniques to keep going. In Embracing the Impossible Obstacle we will identify your block and "cure it" whether it's an Outer Obstacle—family, job, time and place; or an Inner Obstacle—heebie-jeebies, procrastination, lack of belief in yourself.

## How does all this breakdown into 21 days?

First you'll get ready, you'll know who it's about, what it's about, how and where it's going to take place. You'll find a visual aid, brainstorm, know your hero, have the title, the logline and your workspace.

From Day 1 to Day 7 you will write a very fast random draft. We'll show which pages to write each day and what you'll need to cover. You will work for no more than 3 hours on any day (and usually less). That way you can still keep the day job and your life.

On Day 8 you rest.

On Day 9 you read your random draft.

From Day 10 to Day 17 you rewrite. You'll do specific pages each day. We'll tell you which ones and what to do with them.

From Day 18 to Day 21 you tweak and polish.

On Day 21 you celebrate.

The days can be as short as 10 minutes and at no time longer than 3 hours. The 3 hours do not have to be consecutive so that you can break it down into 8- and 10-minute intervals throughout the day.

Not only are we going to make a hard thing simple. We'll also have some fun.

## Random yammerings

Once we get your head out of the way, your heart is free to work on the movie. We'll start with a stream-of-unconsciousness. All you do is dump down everything on the page that you already have in your heart about your movie. This will seem like random yammerings to you. There is power in understanding that random yammerings are actually connected ideas that together create a whole new picture.

Think of a dream. Until you figure out its meaning, it's just a hodge-podge of weird images. But a dream is actually a night movie designed to tell you a story.

## The power of juxtaposition

Here's an example:

>           FRANK
> How's your wife? You haven't brought
> her around lately.

>           RALPH
> She's fine. Did you hear Jack's getting
> a divorce?

From this short exchange, can you guess the relationship between Ralph and his wife? Do you see how seemingly unrelated thoughts placed together tell a story?

With the Inner Movie Method, our first draft is a random draft. There's no anxiety because, after all, this is only a random draft. Then we rewrite from the head. We hone, modify, eliminate. Once our heart produces a random draft, our head can read it to find out what it's about.

Try it with a dream. When you wake up, you ask, "What was that all about?" Your mind tries to make sense of it. But try this —instead; jot down everything you remember. You'll find you remember more and more as you jot. *Later*, look over the random notes and the meaning will hit you. First heart then head and it will all make sense. First you put your socks on then your shoes.

## Acta non verba (actions not words)

This is a participation book. Let's talk. Let's write. Let's do more than read. Let's use color and sound and vision and feeling. Let's create a great movie. Want to?

What we do with the Inner Movie Method is we don't mess with the rational, sensible part of you that knows you can't, you shouldn't, you better not. We go to the part that has to, that must, that is aching to jump right in on behalf of itself. That way we've got the best parts of you working automatically, easily—even when you're sleeping.

## The bicameral significance of the use of lucky socks

This is the place where I was going to give the once and for all scientific explanation of the Inner Movie Method. But here's what: When you go to a movie the writer doesn't appear and tell you about it before you see it. And since we believe in "show, not tell," let's just wham right into it! Because then, in three weeks, when you're at a hot shot Hollywood party accompanied by your finished script and someone asks you, "What is The Inner Movie Method?" you can show them.

So are you ready? All you need is

· a wish to write a movie,
· the idea you don't quite have yet,
· and this book.

Let's go!

How to
Get Ready

## How to start writing your screenplay

(A) You'll need to know what you want to write, and
(B) You'll need to know how to write it.
That's what we'll accomplish in this section.
Before you get to the 21 Days you will know

· What your movie is about.
· Who it's about.
· What the overriding feeling is that you want to convey.

You will have ready

· Your place to write.
· Your time to write.
· Your support from loved ones.
· Your visual aid.
· Your lucky socks.


This is going to be a great movie!

# WHAT TO WRITE

### Where ideas come from

Ideas are the only thing inflation hasn't hit. They're still a dime a dozen. It's what you do with your ideas that gives them value.

You could start with a character, or an issue, or an event from your life or the newspaper. It can be a question you want to explore or a problem you need to solve.

Here's how far you have to look for a story . . . . Look inside yourself. Everything there is to know about Everyman is within every man.

### What's my story
### and how am I going to tell it?

Something happens to someone . . . . You've got to know who and you've got to know what.

You might want to intellectualize your intentions, "I'm doing an allegory on the state of modern man in relation to the inherent dignity of the human soul." That's great. Save it for the interview after your movie is a hit. To write it, think in terms of one man, not mankind. Ask yourself, "Suppose event *x* happens to him. What would my hero do about it?"

## First assignment

What do you know so far about your movie?

Imagine you're in a theater and your movie comes up on the screen. Run it in your head right now. No matter how little you think you know, run it quickly like your life flashing before you.

You might have noticed bits and pieces and surprise images. Did you see that you know more about your movie than you thought? Great!

You might have noticed nothing. That's okay too, because even though you didn't get visual images you probably did get a feeling. We'll be working with that feeling soon. Whatever you saw or felt, this "first assignment" will help to clarify and to focus on an all-important question.

## What am I going to write about?

If you're worried that your idea needs to be commercial, let's take a load off your mind right away. You won't be writing to be commercial or to compete with established writers for *Rambo 12*. You get to write the one script no one else can write. The one story burning to get out of you is your "commercial" script. You can't be a second-class somebody else; you can only be a first class you. You have only one real commodity as a writer— your point of view.

## What is my point of view, and how can I see it?

Your point of view is your unique way of looking at the world based on all your experiences and how you feel about them up to this moment.

Here's an example of how one person sees life differently from another:

Susy and I have been best friends since we were one each.

When we were seven, her cat caught a rabbit and tore at it until we intervened. Our neighbor, Mr. Williams, took it upon himself to "put the rabbit out of his misery" by drowning him in a bucket of water while Susy and I looked on.

Afterward, describing this experience, I said, "Struggling against death, the rabbit drowned in our tears."

Susy said, "Did not. Mr. Williams filled the bucket from the sink in the basement."

It's the same story, but seen from different viewpoints.

So you see, there's no right or wrong way of presenting a movie; there's just P.O.V.

You might ask, "Suppose 'they' aren't buying my particular point of view this year?"

You needn't worry about what "they" are looking to buy, because "they" don't know what they're looking for until they find it.

## How to tell if your idea is a novel, a movie, a play, or a song— and what to do about each

A movie is visual. It tells your story by showing action and re-action. Events occur. Its scope is bigger than one room. Its time and space are elastic. You can go back and forth from the future, to the past, to the present; from today to two thousand years from today; from here, to there, to wherever.

Do you have a story that can be told visually and that hinges on action and external events? Then your story is a movie.

Do you have an issue or a relationship between characters you'd like to explore through in-depth conversation? Then a play would be the best platform for you.

Do you want to climb around in the heart and mind of a character and explore his feelings? Then a novel would serve very well, because in a novel you can write what your characters are thinking.

Do you have a concept—one clear thought that is all that has to be said to cover your subject? Then try a song. A song is a minimovie—a beginning, middle, and end that has a hook, tells a story, makes a point. Many movie ideas could be crystallized into a solid song message.

If you are going to write your story as a screenplay, know that you'll need to use outside events to show inner growth. You get to show, not tell.

## Let's decide what your story is about

Keep asking, "What if?"

Here's a brainstorm session. Read through it and then we'll utilize the technique to brainstorm your story into existence.

My niece Amy asked me to help her. She needed to write a public service spot (commercial) for SADD (Students Against Drunk Drivers). So I said "Okay, let's do it this minute, in the car on the way from the airport."

*Inner Movie Axiom: The moment to start your story is when you don't think you know your story.*


*Viki:* What is the message you want to convey?

*Amy:* "Don't drink and drive."

*V:* And it's directed at teenagers?

*A:* Yes.

*V:* Let's start with time and place. Where along the situation do you want to show it? At the getting drunk time, at the car, at the accident, at the ambulance, at the funeral?

*A:* I don't know.

*V:* Just decide—if it's not right it will lead to what is right.

*A:* At the funeral.

*A:* Whose—the driver or the driver's victim?

*A:* This is for my school, so I don't want to imply any of our students drink. So it's somebody else who hits one of our friends.

*V:* Are the friends standing at the funeral talking about the accident?

*A:* Yes.

*V:* Let's make this stronger. If they are at a funeral talking about what happened, that makes it a hearsay scene. It's old news being talked about. In film we can go directly to action. Let's move it forward or backward. Either to the scene of the accident or. . . . What if they are in the hospital, and the girl-friend of the boy who was killed is just waking up in traction, and her friends are there to tell her that he has died.

*A:* Yeah!

*V:* Okay, is it the girlfriend of a boy or were they two girls or two boys in the car?

*A:* Girlfriend and boyfriend.

*V:* Let's rethink who was drunk. You wanted it to be an outside person who hits our friends. Would it have more impact if it's our friend who was drinking?

*A:* That's probably the hardest situation—for the girlfriend to tell her boyfriend he's drunk. I think I could tell my girlfriend more easily.

*V:* Great! Now you're coming to the core of why it's difficult for a friend to stop a friend from driving drunk.

*A:* I don't want to write that though. I like the hospital.

*V:* Okay, always go with your instinct. (Note where you resist. Sometimes it means you've stumbled on your story but you're not ready to write it yet. Fine. Go around it, that will get you back to it.)

*A:* In the hospital the girlfriend is waking up.

*V:* What's her name?

*A:* Lisa. And the others are a boy and two other girls.

*V:* And their names?

*A:* The first girl is . . .

*V:* Call her Amy. Did you notice how somewhere you already knew she was going to have your point of view? So call her by your own name, to remind yourself that you don't have to invent a new character.

*A:* The others are Chuck and Cindy.

*V:* What are their attitudes?

*A:* Chuck is mad and Cindy cries a lot.

One thing that happens in storytelling is that we tend to start telling the story from far away. For instance, we tell it in hearsay scenes (the funeral) rather than by depicting the action (car crash). We tell it in minor characters (the girlfriend) rather than through the character it really happened to (the drunk driver).

As you decide your story into existence, take giant steps forward by taking the story closer and closer to its true source. *Give the story to the main character.*

*V:* Can we get closer now? Is the girlfriend who the story is about? How about if it's the drunk driver? His friends are there when he wakes up to tell him that Lisa's dead?

*A:* Okay, I've got it. Greg wakes up worried about his car. He doesn't take responsibility.

Notice when the story suddenly begins to come to life.

Jump in and start filling in parts of the picture. When you get to a blank spot, ask yourself a question. Answer it. Keep going.

When Amy was pretty sure she knew the gist of her 60-second story, we did this: She closed her eyes and pictured it while I counted to 60. That gave her a realistic fix on the pace of the thing. Could she cover what she wanted in that time?

Then, there in the car, on the freeway, she wrote it.

### SADD SPOT
#### by Amy Lynn King

FADE IN:

GREG'S P.O.V. - Subjective camera

GREG "sees" his leg in traction, hospital surroundings. LYNN, CHUCK and CINDY are in the room. Chuck is sadly looking out the window. Lynn holds Greg's hand. Cindy's crying. As Greg speaks, Chuck rushes from window.

>                    GREG
>                 (weakly)
>         Hey, guys...So how bad is it? Is my
>         car totalled? God, my dad is going to
>         *kill* me for wrecking that baby. I'm
>         telling you that light on Big Oak Road
>         has gotta get fixed.

>                                        CUT TO:

GREG AND LISA IN CAR - MUSIC ON

A light they approach is yellow, turns red. Greg fumbling from gas to brake.

BACK TO SCENE

>                    GREG
>         If that light wasn't constantly on the
>         blink, none of this would've happened.

                    CHUCK
                   (angrily)
          It wasn't the light, Greg, it was you!
          You were drunk.

                                        CUT TO:


GREG AND LISA, ARM IN ARM, LEAVING A PARTY

                            CHUCK
          Bye.

                            GREG
                           (slurs)
          See ya later.

BACK TO SCENE

                            GREG
          If I was so drunk, why didn't any of
          you stop me from driving?

Lynn, Chuck and Cindy exchange sad looks.

                       GREG (CONT'D)
          Lisa didn't think I was that drunk. She
          was with me. Why don't you ask her?

                                        CUT TO:


CAR CRASH

BACK TO SCENE

                            LYNN
          Greg... Lisa's dead.

REACTION SHOT - GREG

                       ANNOUNCER (V.O.)
          Drunk driving is everyone's responsi-
          bility.

SUPER OVER:

          "STUDENTS AGAINST DRUNK DRIVING"

                  -THE END-

So the way to know your story is to ask yourself questions then answer. Just decide. If it doesn't fit then decide again until it does fit.

## So what's the story?

Can you say what your story is now? Do it in layers. Ask "What if." Take note of everything you know about it so far. What's the beginning, middle, and end? Bits and pieces will come to you. This is the jot stage. Try not to get too detailed yet. Keep looking at the big picture, the overview. Any one scene that's too detailed at this stage can throw the whole out of balance. If a scene does come to you in detail, jot it on a 3x5 card and put it on a "scenes in detail" pile. (Use 3x5 cards because you can't write too much on them.) Keep it simple. Write big, say very little. Paint word pictures: "Night. Storm. Desert." Use nouns. Let the nouns describe the picture; instead of "huge, expensive house," say "mansion."

Jot down now for 8 minutes everything you know so far about your movie.

\\\\\\\\\\\\\\\\\\\\\\\\\\\\\\\\\\\\\\\\\\\\\\\\\\\\\\\

Terrific. Is this exciting or what? You know so much more than you thought you did.

P.S. If you haven't done any of this yet, do it. Getting ready to get ready takes too long. When you just jump in you'll be amazed at how ready you really were.

## Who is it about?

Now let's get acquainted with your hero. Ask questions about him and answer them. If he graduated from high school in the 60s, what year was he born? Does that make him a war baby? Ask your heroine about herself. She will start to talk to you. Notice her tone. Is she mad, scared, free and light?

Be on the lookout for tone. The story is entirely different when the tone changes. Eddie Murphy's role in *Beverly Hills Cop* was initially going to be played by Sylvester Stallone. Think about how different the tone of the film would have been had he starred. Now cast your film. What actor would play your hero?

## Show, not tell

A word here about what a screenplay is not: It is not introspection. We see what characters do, not what they think. Character is revealed through action, and very often; in fact mostly, we humans don't do what we think and don't say what we feel. We don't often act, but act out; that is, we often shout when we really want to cry, say yes when we really mean no. So as screenwriters we have to find ways to show that a character might be doing one thing while meaning something else entirely. We have to find ways for the audience to interpret these actions as we intended. Here's where subtext comes in. Subtext is all the true meaning that is going on underneath the actions.

A great scene to illustrate this is in William Goldman's *Butch Cassidy and The Sundance Kid*. When they are both about to die and we know it, and they know it, and they each know the other knows it. The line is from Sundance and reads something like this:

> SUNDANCE
> The next time you say let's go to Australia, let's go to Australia!

Here are two guys arguing about their future when what's really going on is they're both about to die. This is a line to say goodbye. William Goldman is a master of saying one thing to mean something much deeper.

Here's an assignment. Notice subtext today in your everyday activities: i.e. when the bagger at the supermarket says, "Have a nice day," as he rams the cart across the customer's toes. Find how one scene is being played out while a much deeper meaning emerges.

## Now what?

Chances are by now you have a little of this and a little of that about your story. Now, What is the story? I mean thematically. You may know that your hero is a detective and he's after the murderer, but why is he doing this? Why are you writing this? What's this about?

I'm glad you asked.

## How your age reveals what's on your mind

No matter how different our lives are from one another, we tend to land on specific themes at specific ages.

This works out swell for the Inner Movie Method, because all you have to do is look at your age and you can get insight into the theme of your story. After working with hundreds of people who have written their Inner Movies, I discovered that the themes fall into "Writes of Passage."

Your age theme will be a major key in unlocking your Inner Movie.

## Life is a metaphor

The story that you write will be a metaphor for your life. Your character is you. This doesn't mean your movie has to be about someone who is writing a movie. It means that the life issue that most concerns you now will be explored in your writing.

In storytelling, this happens naturally. We use the particular to illustrate the universal. But the clearer you are about the particular (you), the more powerfully you can tell a story that is true for many.

The themes are specific, the applications are infinite. Therefore once you acknowledge *your* theme, you are empowered to play it out on any situation you choose.

## Writes of passage

Here's a quick checksheet to help you locate your life issue and how it will affect the story you want to write.

### ROCKING AND ROLLING

Let's start at age seventeen. You are probably experiencing a balancing act in which your emotions are catching up the adult circumstances in which you start finding yourself. Your movie can be about first love and how that can hurt *and* be wonderful. You are deciding if all that feeling is worth it.

At nineteen the theme tends to be "So what's the big deal anyway?" You have a certain detached candor in commenting on the world. You will have a strong main character with definite opinions.

### "AM I SPECIAL? I *AM* SPECIAL. I'M NOT SPECIAL."

In the early twenties, it's "I'm okay, and the world is terrible," and then by the late twenties you've evolved to "I'm okay and the world is how it is, now how do we get along together?"

Are you a young woman in your twenties who is struggling to earn enough money? Do you have a car? Chances are your relationship with your father includes the car. This is often the way father-daughter relationships get worked out. You call him when your car breaks down. It breaks down a lot or if it's new your father helps with the payments. This is an important time of ambivalence surrounding finances and love. Is someone going to take care of you or are you going to take care of yourself? You're deciding.

The twenties are the time to shuck excess baggage. You're deciding which beliefs truly belong to you and which were given to you by your upbringing and are dispensable. You do not yet have imperviousness. Things can still get to you and send your emotions spinning. Your movie could be about making the world over so that you'd better like to live in it. There will be "tell-off" scenes. At least one character over thirty will be made to look like a buffoon. You will want to show corruption, good and bad. Your hero will be idealistic. He is being asked to "sell out," but his idealism, against all odds, triumphs.

The twenties are great for discovering what you don't want. You haven't begun to discover what you do want till the middle thirties.

### UNFINISHED BUSINESS

In your early thirties you will have a theme involving your relationship with your mother or father. This is a time to settle the unfinished business of who your parents are versus who you are and what you want to be. If there is a battle *against* your mother and father, it is a battle *for* the self. You want their approval but you think that their approval is only given if you stay a child. But you can't stay a child—you'll die. This is a time to risk growing up and surpassing your parents. Your movie might not necessarily use a mother or father to illustrate this. You might use any authority figure, or even an archenemy. Notice if you're writing a murder mystery. You are extremely angry at your parent and your movie is a way to express that anger.

Thirty is a turning point similar to page 30 in a script. Whatever you were doing until now completely changes, and you are on a different path, particularly in work and in love. You find that something is important to you that wasn't until now.

One of the really interesting times for men is in their early thirties, when they feel an urgency to define their manhood by the age of thirty-five. This is when you feel you must prove yourself. "This is it." "Time is up." "You have to lay it on the line out there." The script you write now tends to be a very good one. Often you have one idea that's smoldering inside, burning to get out (what I refer to as The Big One), but you're not sure if you should write that one or one that's more "commercial." Always go to the strength of The Big One, otherwise you'll bog down at age fifty and have to come back to it then.

Scripts with do-or-die themes are the ones that don't get written, because you think if you don't do it you'll die, but what you learn is that you don't do it and you *don't* die. Once the script teaches you that big lesson, you are ready for your next script, which is "You don't prove nothing till you got nothing to prove." This is usually in your late thirties—actually thirty-seven, when you're beginning to know you're going to be all right.

For women, from thirty-five to forty is a great time for themes of love. You'll be exploring new ways to be in relationships. If your character has been a victim, now's the time she stops. "It's my turn."

By your late thirties, if you haven't done whatever it is you want to do, this is when you do it. You want to "come true" before forty.

### IN FULL BLOOM

Forty is a major time. It's *important* to have become what you've wanted to become. It's a time for assessing your personal value. For instance, a man might buy a sailboat or a sports car to honor his financial achievements. Men need to "make it."

Women's themes at forty are very much concerned with their powerfulness—"strutting your stuff."

And life does begin at forty. There's a loosening of the reins of driving ambition.

Now, it's not so much how you fit in the world, but more what world you create for yourself. How are you contributing to it?

## WHEN THE HECK IS MIDLIFE ANYWAY?

By late forties there are themes reflecting thoughts like "Is what I have become enough?" or "Is that all there is?"

Physically there is a swing between "I'm falling apart" and "I never felt younger." From a writer in her late forties we might get a story about a mother of teenagers who decides to run the marathon. This story encompasses all the issues for this time—physical stamina, achievement, hope. This is also a time to write a story about an affair with a younger lover. Or a cut-loose story where an executive drops out of the corporate jungle and heads for the woods.

## NEW BEGINNINGS

At fifty, you've gone about as far as you can go the old way. Now what?

There's a shift in thinking. You have a taste for a major move, or at least an exotic vacation. Themes for your movie are concerned with exploring new areas. Some of the new areas might be the old ones you left behind along the way. For instance, if you didn't write The Big One when you were in your thirties, you can go back and do it now. This is a time to rewrite your history to have it come out how you want it. If you are a man, your hero is likely to be in his thirties and going through a life test. If you are a woman, you might be experiencing the empty nest syndrome, those feelings that can come over you when the last of your kids are now off to life's new possibilities as you see yours diminishing. This is a wonderful "come alive" time for you. It's "your turn," the one you missed earlier.

I'll tell you about Ruth. She decided to cash her grandmother's bonds and do something special, but she didn't know what. She agreed to make a list of one hundred possible "come alive" activities. The list ranged from buying a thousand yellow roses to getting the carburetor fixed. Several weeks later, I got a postcard from her from the Caribbean: "I'm snorkeling on Grandma's bonds. Love, Ruth."

If you are a woman whose kids have grown up and out, then write about what you know so well. Value it. Don't feel you have to write a detective thriller.

### I AM WHO I AM "AS IS"

If you are in your sixties, your theme will be one of memory. You have a history and have gained the long view. If you feel that you haven't yet done what you wanted to in life, you will have an urgency to "not be buried with it." So your movie can have a quest-and-find theme. But mostly from those in their sixties comes one of my favorite themes: "This is it. This is all there is. And that's everything."

### HORIZONS

Our seventies are a time for putting our lives into perspective. It's a time to ask, "So what was that all about anyway?" Movie themes from screenwriters in their seventies tend to show tremendous perspective on what has true value. Some other themes that are explored include immortality and health.

## Outer circumstances

We can get stuck in an emotional pocket at any age, and this will affect our theme.

For instance, when you are fifty you can go back to settle feelings that arose when your father died when you were ten.

If you are still angry about something that derailed your life some time ago, your theme will reveal a desire for revenge, a hope for redemption, or a righteous indignation. You may want to do an exposé of corruption.

Grief is another strong motivation to write. Do you have a movie about that person and your relationship with him?

## The gender factor

There is a difference between men's and women's approach to theme. Women tend to perceive wholeness in relation to other people, whether it's (a) a need to find others to feel whole, or (b) a decision to find wholeness separate from others. Women's movie themes tend to involve other people. A man tends to perceive wholeness through a test he puts to himself; a test he must ultimately decide whether he's passed. His test tends to pit him against his own life's circumstances. Her test tends to pit her sense of herself against her relationships.

Men tend to be linear. Event *a* causes *b,* therefore *c* happens. Women tend to be lateral. For instance, a wife and mother can make sandwiches, look for the other sock, and carry on a conversation with her husband and the kids at the same time. If the man is home on a Saturday with the kids, he might run the show linearly, doing one thing at a time—the laundry, then the lunches. This is good to know when you approach your characters.

## Your hero

Let's not beat around the bush. Your main character is you. Using the age checklist, ponder for a moment, what is the main issue of your life at this time? What are you questing after? What do you hope to find? See how your wants and needs relate to what your character wants and needs.

## How to make up a true story

*We tend to dismiss what we know and think we need to know what we don't know. Your movie will be, thematically, what you're experiencing for yourself as you sit down to write.*

But whatever you choose to write about, make sure it's the thing that really means something to you. *Inner Movie Axiom: Fiction is a way to tell the truth.*

What you want to say is already waiting to come out of you. You may not know ahead of time why you're writing it or what it means to you, but you will discover its significance as you go.

## Writers ask

*Q:* When we write a script, is it always related to our own lives?

*A:* Yes. You can't help it. It's just naturally going to be you. Screenwriting is a lot of trouble. And if you're only working something out for a fictional character who doesn't exist in some part in you, then it isn't worth it.

*Q:* Then my protagonist is usually going to be me?

*A:* Yes. And you will find that you will keep secrets about your hero. All the other characters will be much clearer because they are "outside" you; the hero or heroine will be less clear, ironically, because he or she is so obviously an extension of some part of you that you know very well. You will reveal your character by telling the truth.

## How to find your central life issue

Have you gotten some insight into what your central life issue is? Based on your age theme, can you now answer, "What am I questing after?"

## Answer these questions

Who is your character? Tell us everything you know about him/her so far.

What does he/she want?

What is he questing after?

Go to yourself. If the character seems to be you—then jump in and *make* him you. In other words, don't hide or camouflage his desires and feelings. The idea is to find and show the real feelings, because they will tell you what is true. *Inner Movie Axiom: There is no writing that is fiction, except maybe bad writing.* Write from your heart. Your heart is smarter than your head. Write the movie that's already starring you.

If you think you don't have a story, ask yourself:

Why did I want to do this?

What is the central question I want to explore?

How do I want the audience to respond to this movie?

Who is the hero?

What does he need?
What does he want?
Why do I want to write this?
Why is this story important to me?
Why do I want to tell this particular story?
What do I think I will learn by exploring this theme?

If you can answer these questions, you're on your way.

## How can I know my characters before I start writing?

Use whatever style that comes naturally to you. Some people will do a 20-page dossier and get very specific about the character's history. This is backstory, and it's a good approach for someone who is *not* character-oriented. The best thing to do as a screenwriter is to keep asking yourself questions about your characters. And then answer.

Just be aware of where your characters come alive for you, and keep picturing them in your mind. Maybe they'll come to you in their statistical facts—birth date, weight, number of kids —or from their personality type—jovial, open. What actor could play him? Find a picture of how he looks. Find an article of clothing he'd wear or some object that would have meaning to him. Write a get acquainted scene between you and your character now.

### How to think cinematically

Let's say you are a first-time screenwriter, and yet you have already read every writing manual and attended every seminar possible. This causes two phenomena: (a) you're still not confident about what to do, and (b) all those concepts are swirling in your mind, confusing you more. It's sort of like trying to tap dance in your head, you have all that theory but your feet are standing still. Let's take concepts such as premise, conflict, and theme and put them in the back of our heads; they'll come up much, much later during rewrite. Now let's lighten up and . . .

# Go to the movies

. . . because (a) you are already an authority on movies, you've seen hundreds of them, and (b) movies will tell you everything you need to know right now. So let's go raise our creative consciousness.

Pick a movie you really want to see and take along your wristwatch. Here's what to look for:

Before you even go into the theater, look over the lobby card (that's the ad in the showcase outside). It will have an illustration and a logline. The logline is the blurb that tells you what it's about (e.g., for *Desperately Seeking Susan*: "A life so outrageous it takes two people to live it"). A logline is often created by the ad department long after everybody on the picture has wrapped and gone home, but it is your first impression of the movie you're about to see. What do you think it's about from the lobby card? Can you see any conflicts in concept here? For instance, there might be several still shots under the lobby card. Do the mood and look of the stills agree with the ad? Try to articulate what you think the story is. Now try to think of a whole different story that this could be advertising. Now think of your movie. What is your logline?

Okay, now go into the theater. Notice the audience. Who came to see this film? What are the demographics—kids, families, couples under thirty-five? What's the genre of the film— action-adventure, romantic comedy? If this is a big-budget, high-concept blockbuster, people are expecting an entertainment event. They will have the large-size bucket of popcorn and pretty much finish eating it before the movie even starts. All this is information for you. Is this the kind of movie you want to write? Who is the audience that's going to come and see your movie? Is it an "important" picture with big stars making big statements? Would you rather your movie be shown in a small art house to a word-of-mouth audience? Here in the theater, decide the type of film that suits you. Already, before the picture has even begun, you have a lot of information about what a movie is. People came here, paid money, and are going to sit in the dark and have a world painted before their eyes. Look at the screen. That's your canvas. What do you want to put up there?

Write down everything you know about *your* movie so far. Notice that you know a great deal.

Now, back to the movie you came to observe.

**FADE IN**

When the movie begins, note the time. Each minute is one page of script, so ten minutes is ten pages; the first half hour is when there is an event ending Act I and beginning Act II. (Do not set your watch. Movie writing is an art form. These are guidelines to help you tell your story the best possible way you can; they are not designed to browbeat the heart out of what you have to tell.)

In the first minute you will know everything there is to know about the movie and whether you're going to like it or not. Eventually, you will get so the instant the movie fades in you will know where the problems are going to be, whether it will do what it thinks it will do, what its point of view is—instantly.

By the way, what we are doing here is becoming aware of picture making so that you can write a better movie. You are not in the business of being a critic. Try not to judge or criticize what's happening, just note if an action works or doesn't work. Keep asking yourself questions: Do I know what the story is yet? Did I need to be shown more in that scene? Do I know yet who the story is about?

**IN THE FIRST MINUTE**

You will see a place and a time and a mood (a monastery, winter, ominous.) Is it a big picture—overture and large vistas? Maybe it's a little picture about relationships with close-up pans of snapshots on a dresser. The size and scope and feeling will be revealed right away.

What's the pace? Is it James Bond or Indiana Jones in an exhilarating hijinx? These are teasers, two or three minutes of razzle-dazzle that gets you excited but may not have anything to do with the storyline. If you are writing a crime movie, you might want to put the commission of the crime on the first page.

In the first minute you'll see the point of view. In Clint Eastwood movies, "this is a dirty world and somebody's got to make it safe for the rest of us," so we are shown seamy streets and bad guys. Horror movies establish an easily recognizable environment so that when the terrible thing happens we feel the threat. For example, in *Psycho* Alfred Hitchcock chose to have Janet Leigh stabbed to death in a shower. If it had been in a limo, it would have been frightening only to rich people.

Are we getting information? Are we being introduced to characters? What is the hero's attitude toward his surroundings? What attitude are we being asked to accept? If it's a comedy there should be a joke right away that's characteristic of the humor of the whole film. Is it there?

These are just a few of the elements to look for on page 1. What else can you find? Check your watch, realize all the information you've been given in one minute.

Now you know to begin *your* story on page 1. You'll show us a place and time and mood.

If a movie is working, we will also know who it's about; we don't have to know *what* it's about until page 3.

### WHAT'S ON PAGE 3?

Tell us what the movie will be exploring thematically for the next two hours. In *Chinatown*, Robert Towne had Gittes say, "You have to be rich to get away with murder."

Can you find a line of dialogue on page 3 that introduces a central question? Every scene after this builds on that central question.

### WHAT HAPPENS FROM 3 TO 10?

Notice how long it takes for the movie to get the audience's attention. There's a point where the audience will engage as a collective body—is it on the first joke, the first gasp? Has it happened yet? Note if it ever happens. Note if there is dissension in the audience. At what point did the audience not believe?

### EVERYTHING WE NEED TO KNOW BY PAGE 10

Ask yourself these questions: What's the story about? Whose story is it? What does he or she want? What's stopping him from getting it? Do I like her? Do I care if she gets what she wants? Am I wondering what happens next?

If the movie hasn't set up who and what and where by page 10, it will start to lose the audience. Notice if the audience is fidgeting.

From page 10 to page 30, we want to be shown new information based on the challenge presented on page 10. We have to see what our hero is after, and we have to see that it's a problem for him to get it.

Let's start to be aware of scenes now. Maybe the film starts out beautifully, does everything right, but twenty minutes into it you see a scene that doesn't move the story along. In other words, it seems that it didn't give any new information or introduce any new character, and maybe it's telling you something that you already knew from an earlier scene. We should enter a scene at the last best moment; that is, if you want character A to slap character B, don't have A pull up in the car, enter the building, ride up in the elevator, and so forth. Just CUT TO the slap. There is a difference between movement and action. If pulling up in the car has nothing to do with furthering the story, don't use it. In comedy, a cut from scene to scene can be used as a punch line. In *Tootsie*, the agent tells Michael he will "never get a job in this town." CUT TO: Michael dressed as Dorothy going to the audition.

### THE ACT I TURNING POINT

You are now thirty minutes into the film. An event is about to happen that will send the hero on a new pathway into Act II. What is that event? What action is the hero forced to react to?

### THE ACT II METAPHOR

See if you can identify the page 45 scene. This is usually a small scene with symbolic overtones. (If it's a young girl growing up, we see the teddy bear abandoned face down on the window seat next to the cosmetics.) This scene gives us a clue to the resolution.

### THE POINT OF NO RETURN

Notice that when the audience rustles around, you're at a break in action. This is usually after the hero commits further, against all odds, to his goal. This is page 60. After the page 60 scene, there should be a lighter moment, which doesn't necessarily further the action, but gives the audience a breather from the action. This is a good opportunity to show how the hero is changing. Can you identify that scene? From here, the obstacles should begin to escalate.

### A NEW DEVELOPMENT

By page 75, even though the hero is committed to his goal, it looks as if he's not going to achieve it. He's about to give up. How is this handled? How would you write this scene? On page 90, an event occurs that "educates" the hero. He's going to be getting something more than or something different from what he set out to get. (This point is important: if all he gets in the end is what he wanted in the beginning, he hasn't changed. This would seem a lot of trouble for nothing. Let the hero learn something and be changed by what he's going through.) Has he changed? How would you show his growth? Are new complications in the situation presenting themselves to the hero?

### CLIMAX

The Act III event raises the stakes. The hero is very close. He can see his goal. But now he is faced with the final obstacle. He is faced with having to give up everything he has left behind in pursuit of his goal. This builds to a crisis point that puts all he has in jeopardy of being lost. It comes down to the final moment —all or nothing. And because of his final action, he wins or loses and is changed. Has this happened? Are you rooting for him? Does the ending surprise you?

### THE END

What just took place? How do you feel? Did the movie answer the central question it posed? Are you satisfied with the resolution? What is your overriding emotion as the credits roll? What did you learn?

I hope your movie-watching pleasures just increased tenfold.

PS. Among your favorite movies will be those that miss every one of these guideposts and yet they touched you deeply and affected you profoundly. If *your* goal is to touch your audience deeply and affect them profoundly, you will. And the more crafts-manship you are aware of, the better your chances.

Okay. Now go home. We're going to do something with that logline you wrote.

## Logline

Your logline is your story reduced to an ad copy blurb that tells what your movie is about and makes us want to see it.

Look in the theater section of your newspaper now. See the movie ads. Study the loglines. Here are some from past movies.

- *Down & out in Beverly Hills*: "See what happens when a dirty bum meets the filthy rich."
- Goldie Hawn's *Wildcats*: "Her dream was to coach high school football. Her nightmare was Central High."
- *The Money Pit*: "For everyone who's ever been deeply in love or deeply in debt."

I chose these because they are big hits at the local video store. Go in and visit the lobby cards on the wall. (Unfortunately, individual packaging of video cassettes doesn't always include the logline, but otherwise they are a great source of study.) Go ahead, watch *Casablanca*. Play it again.

Let's create two characters and then ask a logline question and see if we can come up with a story for them.

She is career-oriented, successful financially, but bankrupt emotionally. He is solid spiritually but has no material wealth.

Here's the logline: "She has everything but nothing. He has nothing but everything. Together can they have it all?

You see how a logline can crystallize the question you will explore.

Work out your logline now.

~~~~~~~~~~~~~~~~~~~~~~~~~~~~~~~~~~~~~~~~~~~~~

### VISUAL AID

Now you're going to give yourself a present. You know your story vaguely. Perhaps at least enough to identify the feeling you want to evoke. You're going to go shop now for an object that represents that feeling to you.

Have you ever tried to tell someone about a terrific experience and ended up frustrated, saying, "I can't explain it" or "You had to be there"? Well, your job is to take them there. And the way you can do that is by first rekindling the original feeling of being there for yourself and then finding words that fit that feeling, so you can explain it to others.

How we rekindle that feeling is by having handy an object that is loaded with emotion for us. It could be a lucky penny or a rock from the beach. If it's a story about your grandfather, maybe you can find his hat in the cedar chest.

If it's an historical piece about a grandam on a plantation, find a candlestick from the period. If your story came to you while listening to music in a restaurant, get a matchbook from the restaurant and a record of the song.

Find a sensory aid that opens your memory to a feeling. Maybe a color sparks something in you.

As you work on your movie you can continually use your sensory aid to evoke the original feeling you want to portray.

### TITLE

Let's name your script. A working title that serves best is one that continues to give you a visual image (e.g., *The Maltese Falcon*) or a sense of place (*Casablanca*). If you are unsure of your action, use a verb in the title or describe the occurrence (*Raiders of the Lost Ark*, *Harry and Walter Go to New York*).

You don't want a "perfect" title just yet. Because if you have a perfect title, your movie has no new place to go. A good working title is one that is a useful tool to help you write the movie. You can rewrite the working title *after* the movie becomes what it is.

Do this; fill in the blanks:

My hero's name is _____

He/she wants _____

He/she needs _____

In one word, my story is about _____

Great. Everything you need at this point on *what to write* you now have. Next? How to write it.

# HOW TO WRITE

### Blood, sweat,
###   and structure

Now that you know who and you know what, let's deal with how.

You'll want to know how to structure your script. Welcome to the 9-Minute Movie. It will show you what goes on pages 1, 3, 10, 30, 45, 60, 75, 90, and 120 of *your* movie.

### The 9-minute movie

Picture this. You're going to hang a ten-foot tablecloth on a clothesline to dry. If you put a clothespin at one corner and a clothespin at the other corner, you'd have this sagging mass of 120 inches in-between. Now imagine this immense tablecloth is wet and unwieldy and the wind is blowing. That feeling is a little of how you might be feeling as a screenwriter when you look down the line of 120 minutes to fill from the start of your movie to the end. So the thing you need to do is use more clothespins. And you'll want to put them at strategic places along the clothes-line to hold up the tablecloth evenly end to end.

That's what the 9-Minute Movie is—clothespins. *We're going to support your movie at nine points from end-to-end so that it holds to a linear line.*

## Acts

First of all, there are three acts in a movie. Act I is from page 1 to page 30. Act II is pages 30 through 90. And Act III is pages 90 through 120. (We break a movie down into Acts to clarify beginning, middle, and end. Act I is the setup; Act II is the story played out; Act III is the resolution.)

Picture the tablecloth and put clothespins at each end (1 inch and 120 inches) and at 30 inches in from each end. So now it's divided into segments of 30 inches, 60 inches, and 30 inches. That's Act I, Act II and Act III.

It still sags in the middle. So put a clothespin exactly in the middle, 60 inches from each end.

Because of the weight of the middle, it's still sagging a bit between 30 and 60 and between 60 and 90, so put clothespins at 45 inches and 75 inches.

This particular tablecloth has some embroidery along the left end, that's 10 inches deep, so put a clothespin 3 inches in and a clothespin 10 inches in because if this part sags out of whack, the whole tablecloth could be ruined.

Your tablecloth should look like this:

| 1 | 3 | 10 | 30 | 45 | 60 | 75 | 90 | 120 |
|---|---|----|----|----|----|----|----|-----|

That's the 9-Minute Movie. Solid support on pages 1, 3, 10, 30, 45, 60, 75, 90, and 120. Now let's do an instant replay of what goes on each page.

## The 120-page marathon

You know that your movie will be 120 pages long. It will be divided into three acts.

Act I, from page 1 to page 30, is where you'll set up the story by introducing the main characters and situation.

On page 1 you start the story, giving mood and tone and place.

By page 3, we need to know the central question that you'll be exploring throughout the movie.

By page 10, you'll need to tell us what the story is. Keep

setting up more and more information so that we know what the hero wants.

On page 30 an event will occur that moves the hero into new territory. Now, what he wants is challenged, and he has to react to the event.

Act II is from page 30 to page 90. This is where the hero meets with obstacles to what he wants.

On page 45 we see the initial growth of your character. We're told where we'll be going from this point on.

By page 60, the middle of Act II, your hero is in big trouble, and he reaffirms and makes a deeper commitment to what he wants.

By page 75 it looks as if all is lost, and there's even a scene where the hero is just about to give up, then something happens that changes everything—an event that gives him a chance at a goal he didn't even know he had, something he *needed* all along, while until now he has been going after something else.

With Act III, from page 90 on, the resolution of the problem starts, and by page 120 the audience is satisfied that you gave them the story you promised on page 10.

## Here's the single most freeing factor in scriptwriting

Our minds think structure is a scaffolding that our character climbs around in. Like this:

But this is not so.
Structure *is* Character

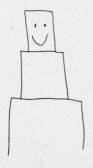

Your character is your story. The events in your screenplay are going to happen as a result of *who* your character is. Your character invents his own reality, therefore any circumstances that befall him are circumstances he brought to himself as a result of how he views the world. So all the events in your movie are going to be external circumstances that manifest what is going on inside your character. Read on to see how the story's structure is really a chronicle of your character's growth.

## Coming alive on cards

Get nine 3x5 index cards. We're going to do the 9-Minute Movie for *your* movie. That way when you begin your 21 Days you will have a 9-card map that will get you through it.

### STORY STARTS ON PAGE 1.

This is it. This is where your movie begins. Now, you may think, "Of course it does!" But you'd be surprised at how much warming up movies do before they get going. You've seen dozens of movies where you're sitting there waiting for the picture to decide what it wants to be about. Yours is not going to do that. Yours is going to begin at the beginning. So on page 1 we need to see the place, the time, and the mood.

This first image comes easily. Take the first image that comes to you.

Now write the image on card #1:

Page one.
INT. SAILBOAT - NIGHT

**What You Have to Tell Us by Page 3.** On card #2 write the central question that you will state on the bottom of page 3. This is the main issue that your screenplay will explore and try to answer.

**Everything We Need to Know by Page 10.** What's the story? What character did you choose to explore the question in what way? Write one line of dialogue on card #3 that tells us who wants what. This line will be on page 10.

**Who Are These Guys and What are You Going to Do with**

**Them on Page 30?** The event that happens on page 30 throws your character a curve. He is forced to respond or react. He might make a plan. He decides on a goal to pursue because of what's happened. He is now going about making the plan and implementing it. Let's see the page-30 event that he is forced to respond to. Then let's see what he plans to do about it, and let's see him taking action according to his plan. Write the event on card #4.

**Moving Forward on Page 45.** On page 45 let's see the start of your character's growth. Write an idea for a scene that would reveal this growth on card #5.

**This Is It.** By page 60 the hero has to commit wholeheartedly to what he wants. He's said what it is he wants in Act I and taken action to that end on page 30, and then we see that he is changing and the circumstances are changing, but the stakes get higher here. He sees it's going to take everything he has to do this—it's harder than he thought—but somehow because it is harder he wants it more. On card #6 state what he commits to by the middle of your story.

**How Our Hero Changes on Page 75.** By page 75 it looks like all is lost; there's even a scene where your hero is just about to give up. But then something happens that changes everything: an event that gives him a chance at a goal he didn't even know he had. Think of such an event and write it on card #7.

**What Happens Next.** Page 90 is the start of the finish. Write on card #8 what the resolution is.

**Going All the Way.** Card #9 is the outcome; the resolution to your story where we see your hero's new life. Give us the ending.

The hardest cards will be #2 and #7. It's okay if these are shaky. If you knew them already you wouldn't have to write the movie. You'll discover these elements as you write.

Just keep going.

## What's it supposed to look like on the page?

### WHAT TECHNICAL STUFF WILL I NEED TO KNOW?

FADE IN:

INT. YOUR HOUSE - DAY

YOU are about to sit down at the typewriter. Suddenly
you get very nervous.

                    YOU
          What is it supposed to look like on the
          page? Do I put in all the camera an-
          gles? Do I have to write everything
          everybody says?

                    INNER MOVIE
          First time screenwriters are usually
          terrified of screenform. It's understand-
          able. You've seen plenty of movies on
          the screen, have you ever seen one on
          paper?

                    YOU
          No, I haven't. This is the first time,
          and you know ... it looks really simple.

                    INNER MOVIE
          The next part is called The 2-Page Pic-
          ture Show. It's filled with tabs, caps,
          cut-to's, and colons. What you'll do is
          sit down and type it.

                    YOU
          You mean that's it. That's everything
          I'll need to know about screenplay
          form?

                    INNER MOVIE
          Guaranteed. You'll be an old hand at
          all this fade-in and cut-to business in
          the time it takes you to type the pages.

                    YOU
          I can't believe it. That was the thing
          that worried me the most, and it's that
          simple?

### INNER MOVIE
The Inner Movie goes to a lot of trouble to make you a technical expert...
simply and effectively. The point is,
once you know the form, you're free to
get to the good part, which is to write
the movie that's playing in you.

You breathe a sigh of relief as we

                                    FADE OUT.

Here's where to set your tabs. Do it now:

FADE IN:

INT. YOUR WORKSPACE - DAY

This is stage direction. Begin it two inches in from left
edge of paper.

                    CHARACTER NAME
        Character names are centered at four
        and a half inches in from the left. Dia-
        logue goes here, three inches in from
        left. Dialogue shouldn't extend beyond a
        line two and a half inches from the
        right edge of the paper.

EXT. COURTROOM - DAY

Here is where you describe what we *see*. If you want to
show a man, write "wealthy, sad executive," or perhaps
"vagrant." These are both men, but the choice of words
makes them two very different men. You can't say "divorced man" because we can't see divorcedness. We can
see "executive" in what the man wears, what he carries,
where he is.

Double space between dialogue and scene description.

                                CHARACTER NAME
                        (astonished) - in paren-
                        theses is an actor's in-
                        struction; don't overuse it.
                This is where you write the dialogue.
                Everything that is said goes in the dia-
                logue.


                                                        CUT TO:


    When you want to stop one scene and go to the next scene,
you can CUT TO or DISSOLVE TO, and you put these indications
on the right.


                                                    DISSOLVE TO:


    If a character isn't finished talking by the bottom of a page,
try to interrupt his speech at the end of a whole sentence. Write
(MORE) on the line beneath the last sentence, indented to align
under the character's name; repeat the character's name and
(CONT'D) on top of the next page.


                                CHARACTER NAME
                    This is how dialogue is split when it
                    will not fit all on one page.
                                (MORE)


(Bottom of page)
- - - - - - - - - - - - - - - - - - - - - - - - - - - - - - - - - - - - - - - - - - - - - - - - - - - - - - - - - - - - - -
(top of new page)


                                CHARACTER NAME (CONT'D)
                    This way the actor knows there is
                    more to come.

**WHEN TO USE CAPS**

    Use caps for the character's name in the stage direction the
first time he enters the script. This is to alert the casting director.
Also, use caps for sound effects, to alert the sound man. (Use
camera angles *only* when absolutely necessary to indicate point

of view). You do not have to cap secondary characters who do not speak (as in crowd scenes) or props. If you must emphasize something in action or dialogue, underline it.

**SOME MISCELLANEOUS USES FOR CAPS.**

AD LIB: when the actors fill in the dialogue with incidental lines.

VOICE OVER (V.O.): when we hear narration over the action.

OFFSCREEN (O.S.): when we hear the character speak but he is offscreen, such as calling out from the other room.

BEGIN TITLES: when the main credits start.

END TITLES: when the main credits finish.

FREEZE FRAME: which is at left margin and punctuated with a period.

TITLES OF SONGS AND BOOKS

## A picture is worth a thousand words

*Inner Movie Axiom: There are no words in a screenplay.*

There is dialogue and there is description, but your writing shouldn't show. You can't say, "There was something chilling about the abandoned mansion, alone at the top of the hill." What you do is show it in a night storm through flashes of lightning. That's how we know it's haunted.

The "writing" is in choosing one image to put next to another so that a picture can be worth a thousand words. That way you don't have to say the thousand words.

## The 2-page picture show

Now you get to write the 2-Page Picture Show. Here's the story. Skeeter Mooch is charged with a second-degree screenwriting felony: excessive camera movement.

Let's start together and then you'll take over:

FADE IN:

EXT. CAR CHASE - DAY

Jalopy careens over bridge onto freeway. COPS in pursuit.

INT. JALOPY - DAY

SKEETER MOOCH, 25, floors it.

CUT TO:

EXT. FREEWAY - DAY

Cops gaining on jalopy. Head it off. Cops run to pull Skeeter from car.

CUT TO:

CLOSE ON SKEETER'S FACE

>                         SKEETER (V.O.)
>           I'm guilty.

CAMERA PULLS BACK TO REVEAL Skeeter in defendant's circle, wrists shackled. He faces JUDGE COOPER.

>                         JUDGE COOPER
>           Skeeter Mooch. Do you have anything
>           to say before sentencing?

>                         SKEETER
>           How do I write out a phone conversa-
>           tion?

Phone RINGS. Judge Cooper answers it.

>                         JUDGE COOPER
>           Judge Cooper here.

INTERCUT PHONE CONVERSATION:

>                         JUDGE'S AGENT
>           Coop, I got interest in your script at
>           Fox.

                    JUDGE COOPER
            Not now, Jaws. I'm sentencing...Have
            your girl call my girl. Let's do sushi.

END ON JUDGE COOPER

                    JUDGE COOPER (CONT'D)

   Now you finish. Keep going until it feels easy. Remember,
everything that's seen goes in description, everything that's said
goes in dialogue.

                                        FADE OUT.

                    THE END

   There. That's all you need to know. Don't try to make it any
harder. There's plenty of time for that later.
   NOTE: If you absolutely must know every reason and why-for
of script formatting, consult *The Complete Guide to Standard
Script Formats, Part 1, The Screenplay*, by Cole and Haag, pub-
lished by CMC Publishing (1980), available through Samuel
French's Theatre and Film Bookshop, 7623 Sunset Boulevard,
Hollywood, California 90046, (213-876-0570). Or, best of all, get
a script of a film you've seen and type it. You will be so smart
you'll know everything.

# WHAT YOU KNOW SO FAR

You've done the 9-Minute Movie. You know generally where you're going. Pages 75 and 90 might be quite vague. That's okay. If you knew before you got there, you wouldn't have to go there. You probably *do* see the outcome you'd like on page 120.

Now let's do a dress rehearsal, casting YOU AS A SUCCESSFUL SCREENWRITER.

### Time and place starring you

Have you arranged a workspace? (If you haven't, check the Impossible Obstacle section under time and place.) Let's try out your workspace with a test sitting. Does it feel right? Can you reach the paperclips? Is there enough light? Will it be quiet at the time you've designated for your writing? Is this the time for you to work, or are you tired or hungry? Write for eight minutes, responding to the question "Am I happy with this place at this time?"

Write now.

Eight minutes later: Read what you wrote. Underline anything that stands out. If anything in your workspace needs changing, change it. Don't resign yourself to live with it. Have this place and time exactly how you need it. Now put on your lucky socks.

Let's invite your movie in.

## How to hold a movie in your hand

This is fun. It requires supplies. Gather together three brass brads and 121 pieces of clean typing paper with three-ring holes.

The first piece of paper will be the title page of your movie. In the center of the page, type your movie title. Don't panic if you don't have a title, now is the time to make one up. This is a working title. It can be changed. In fact, it probably will be changed. Remember, if the title is too solid, too locked in at this point, it doesn't necessarily serve you well, because your script needs room to grow where it wants.

The title page will have on it:

YOUR TITLE

Written
by
(your name)

On the top of the next page type this:

FADE IN:

On the bottom of the very last page, type this:

FADE OUT.

THE END

## The 120-page pile up

Now, put the title page on top, then the FADE IN page, then 118 pieces of blank paper, and then the FADE OUT page on the bottom.

This is your movie. You've created the "space" for it, now all it has to do is move in.

At this juncture, you may experience an uncontrollable urge to pick out a front and back cover in a well-thought-out color. Go ahead, if you must (the whole point of the Inner Movie Method is to celebrate instincts). But here is why the cover is better left as a treat for when you finish: if you decide on a cover now, it gives the script a personality that might not suit the story you have yet to tell.

There's another reason to just have the title page on top: you want to see "Written by" and your name.

Now that you have a 120-page blank movie, let's start filling in the blanks. (As you progress through the 21 Days, replace the blank pages with filled pages.)

Take your cards now from The 9-Minute Movie and read through them. Visualize your movie.

Now you're going to visualize it again right away. This time you're going to number the pages of your 120-page pile, visualizing your movie again as you go. You may number by hand; it's easier than typing. Use the upper right-hand corner and number all the way from page 1 to page 120; see your movie as you do this.

Congratulations! You've now screened your movie for yourself three times. Don't worry if you can only glimpse bits and pieces. If you ran the movie you saw last week at the Bijou through your inner projector now you would probably see about as much as you just saw of your own, and yours isn't even on paper yet. So you're doing very, very well.

## The 9-page pull together

What you will do now is start with page 1 and write (in pencil), near the top of the page under FADE IN: three descriptive words that show the place, time, and mood of your movie (e.g., "mustangs, canyon, dawn"). Just three words, no more.

On the bottom of page 3, write a line of dialogue that represents the central question you will be exploring.

There is no right or wrong page-3 statement. It only needs to be stated here—the rest of the script has the task of proving or disproving it.

Continue now and transfer what you have on your nine cards onto pages 10, 30, 45, 60, 75, 90, and 120.

### Inner theater

Now you've run your movie many different times through your inner projector. Put the brads in your movie and hold it in your hand. It's beginning to come alive.

This is amazing. Look how ready you are—story, character, structure, format, acts, and even a blank movie, ready to be filled. One more thing . . . .

### The 8-minute bad-writing polka

Here's the assignment. Don't think about this. Find a pencil and paper and an object in the room—any object, just decide. Now, write for eight minutes as much as you can about that object. You have to tell everything there is to know about it in eight minutes or banshees will come to your door and sell you a vacuum cleaner. One other thing: you are allowed to write badly —extremely badly. You are required to please play the fool. Ready? Go!

Eight minutes later:
Okay, time's up.
Here's what you might have noticed:

1 That was easy to do.
2 Even though you might have resisted at first, *something happened*, and you got interested.
3 You know more about that object than you realized.

And here's the main point:

**4** The assignment was to write badly. Read it. It's not bad. In fact, parts are even brilliant. Underline the brilliant parts. Do you notice something about them? Do you notice they aren't about the object, that they're about you?

Here's what to learn from this:

**1** Writing is not hard.
**2** Good writing is so easy it's accidental.
**3** It's no accident that good writing is personal.

## Multiple choice

Answer these questions now: Are you ready? Do you want to jump right into your 21 Days?

If you answered yes, go directly to the next part.

But if you don't feel ready yet, go to "Embracing the Impossible Obstacles," (on page 131) get the obstacles out of your way, and then come back to the 21 Days part.

## All you need to know
## before you write your random draft

Answer this checklist:

Do I have a *sensory aid*? Something that evokes the feeling of my story?

*Place*: Do I have a writer's place to work?

*Time*: Have I decided on a writing time for each day and made an appointment with myself?

*Form*: Have I typed the 2-Page Page Picture Show? Am I satisfied that I have a feel for the form (i.e., for what is dialogue and what is description)?

*Content*: Can I state what I think my story is in a logline? (If not, do it now quickly. Don't think, just jot it down.) Can I state the question I'd like the story to answer? Can I tell the story in three short sentences (beginning, middle, end)? Can I state my purpose for writing it?

Ready *or not*—go forward.

Let's write Your Movie . . . .

# TRANSITION
# FROM "GETTING READY"
# TO "GO"

Imagine you're on a talk show to plug your movie. You have three minutes to tell us what it's about.

Write for three minutes now: "My movie is about . . . ."

Great!

Also on this talk show we're going to get to see a one-minute clip from your movie. Choose a one-minute clip now. Set it up for us in a few sentences. Explain where it appears in the context of the movie. Now run the one-minute clip on your inner projector.

Welcome to Hollywood. You have created an entire promotional campaign for a movie that you're going to start writing tomorrow.

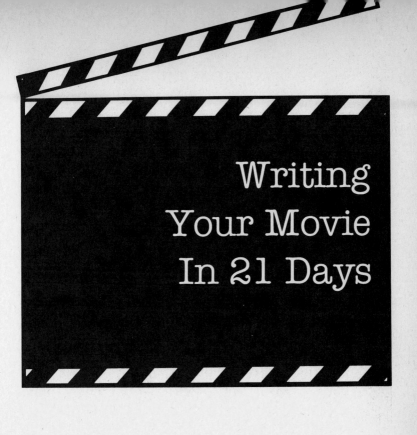

Writing
Your Movie
In 21 Days

# YOUR RANDOM DRAFT;
# WRITE FROM YOUR HEART

## DAY 1: THE FIRST 10 PAGES

Are you ready?

You know your story—vaguely. You can state it in two or three sentences. You can give the logline. You know your main characters and the place. You're ready. Welcome to the random draft.

If you have been thinking about your movie for some time, chances are you envision a very detailed opening that you have played in your head down to the last meticulous gesture. When you sit down to put it into movie form, you might immediately go catatonic because you think, "How do I get her from the table to the stove and back again?"

Here's a sample of how you might think it should be done.

FADE IN:

INT. SUE AND MAX'S KITCHEN - MORNING

EXTREME CLOSE UP (ECU) of two fried eggs cooking. CAMERA PULLS OUT TO REVEAL SUE, a young housewife, newly married, cooking breakfast. She is wearing her plaid robe. It's 8 A.M. She's late for work. She's a bank teller. She realizes her boss will be mad. She pours orange juice as she worries about being on time and rushes to make sandwiches for lunch even though she's on a diet. The eggs are ready.

> SUE
> (shouts to Max)
> Honey, the eggs are ready.

She puts them on a plate and then walks to the table as she shouts:

> SUE
> (to Max)
> I'm putting them on the table.

MAX enters in plaid robe. Crosses to Sue and kisses her neck.

> SUE
> You're not dressed.

> MAX
> (lustfully)
> No, I'm not.

Notice two things: (a) there is information that can't be shown (her boss being mad) and (b) there are redundant instructions (for her to walk to the table, for instance, when the dialogue already demands this action). A script is (a) description, what we see, and (b) dialogue, what is said. Find ways in your story using what we'll see and what is said.

Here's a better way to write that scene:

INT. KITCHEN - MORNING

SUE cooks breakfast. MAX enters. Caresses Sue.

> SUE
> Mmmm.

> MAX
> Mmmm.

They sink to the floor in the folds of matching thick
robes.

Do you see how much easier that is? Do you see how the
scene gets right to its purpose?

Write it in master scenes. That means seeing the action as
though you were a spectator in the room. Let the director put in
close-ups and inserts of her reaction and his hand on the toast.
I put that last part there about the folds of their matching robes
because I wanted to suggest lovemaking as opposed to lust.
New marriage. A kind of innocent commitment. There's something about matching robes that's going to be challenged in this
story.

Once you're writing in spartan form, when an image comes
to you, you can recognize it and it's a clue to your story.

What we're after here is an overall feeling. Think of this draft
as a sculptor would work on a slab of clay, first shaping it
roughly. Set an overall feeling. Later you will hone details. If you
work out small details now, you'll end up with a slab of clay with
one perfect eye looking out of it.

The random draft is for discovery. You are mining for riches.
You'll be amazed at what wonders will appear.

Here's the plan: Write the random draft. Read it. Find out
what your movie is about. Rewrite by taking out everything that
isn't your movie.

So the task of the random draft is to show you the movie you
want to write.

Now you are at the typewriter, wearing your lucky socks, so
you have objects around that remind you of the characters. You
are familiar with how a movie looks on paper. Your tabs are set.
If you are writing in longhand, you've already determined how
many of your handwritten pages equal a typed page.

### SPEED PAGES

The plan is to throw down an image on the page as fast as
you can. As fast as it comes to you, that's how fast you want to
tell us what pictures you're seeing.

You are not writing your movie today; you are only dashing
down the first ten pages of the random draft. You're just going

to give a feeling, and it's a feeling you already know. You don't have to think anything up. Just give us what you feel.

Write like a madman. Dump out everything you know about your idea. It doesn't have to make sense, just dump it as though it were a hot coal and it had to be gotten out of you before it burned a hole.

Results for today are measured by your page count. Dash down ten speed pages and you get an Oscar for outstanding presentation by a speedwriter for Day 1.

You have two hours. You can actually do ten speed pages in ten minutes, but you have two hours. You can get it done in the first ten minutes and go celebrate, or you can take the whole time.

### RULE 1 AND RULE 2

Rule 1: Ten pages or two hours, whichever comes first. If you don't have ten pages after two hours, you broke Rule 2.

Rule 2: Don't think.

Take a deep breath. Imagine yourself in a theater. Your movie comes up on the screen. Write what you see.

### SPECIAL BONUS CRISIS INTERVENTION

Help! Help! I need more help!

There will be some questions that occur to you as you go. Should I start in the car or have a scene before that, in the house? Should I have him be an ex-con? These questions come up, so you can answer them. They are not there to stop you. Make decisions—keep taking action. Okay, she likes him. Play out that scene; if it doesn't work, then try it another way. She doesn't like him. What serves your story best?

Here's what decision making is: *powerful*! You are creating a world. Keep going when you get to a question. Decide and write it in. Don't worry about the best thing to say—that's later. Just get them in the room. Just get them going on action and the story.

It will come at you and leave you in waves. "I got it! I got it!" "The whole thing is in my head and I'll just dash it down." *And then*; "Oh no, this is too hard," "It's too much," "I can't handle it." All emotions will happen. Excitement. Elation. Panic. You need all these parts of yourself to establish your story's depth and width and breadth. Jump. Just jump. *Inner Movie Axiom: It's only a risk if you don't take it.*

Besides, you're not alone. Your characters will actually talk to you. They'll tell you, "Turn the fire up," "Come on in deeper," "Don't go away." Look at your dialogue. What are your characters telling you to do?

"Talk to me. Don't just stand there."

Your characters will always ask you for more life. Give it to them.

### WRITERS ASK

*Q:* I know I'm supposed to set the mood and establish the characters on page 1. How do I do that?

*A:* Here's how to get all that on your page 1 . . . . Forget it, it's in the back of your mind already—all you have to do is make a few decisions. Who is your movie about? Where does it take place? What's the story? Close your eyes. Images will come to you. *That* is your first page. Now write it down as you see it.

*Q:* I have so many questions. Should my character be mad or start crying? Is he thirty-two or seventeen?

*A:* Here's what the creative process is: forming questions that cause answers that in turn lead to better questions.

Let's say every time you don't know something about the script you ask a question. This has two effects: (a) it immediately identifies what it is you don't know, and (b), since you have now identified what you don't know, you are much more able to find out. The first part is the key. In writing, you have to keep identifying what you don't yet know so that you can create it. (What if my character's twenty-two instead of twenty? Then he'd be graduating. That's great! It makes his actions more urgent.)

Keep asking questions and then answer quickly. To write is to make decisions (Okay, he's twenty-two, let's see what that does to his relationship with her. What if she's older than he is?)

Ask yourself what has to happen in this scene. And then

what? And *then* what? Write quickly. Do not elaborate. It's just a map to get you where you're going. Any holes or changes are a lot easier to fix once you see them on the page.

*Q:* It was going great, then I went blank. Why?

*A:* What you might find is that you get a detailed first three pages and then you keep refining it, chiseling it in stone. This is an exercise in trying to tell yourself you can do it. You can. You will. Move on. Remember you are writing the first draft first, and all the first draft does is let you know what you already know but don't yet know you know.

*Q:* Would you repeat about structure?

*A:* By the bottom of page 3, we need to know what story you're going to be showing us. After page 3 you continue to give us more and more information. You are setting up your story all along. You are telling us who this is about. Where we are. What the main character wants to have. On the bottom of page 10, you state clearly what the story is. Page 3 is the theme—we're going to explore the possibilities of love between an older woman and a younger man. On page 10 it's about this woman and this man in this situation and what they both want. You don't need anything else today.

If you haven't done your speed pages, do them now.

### I DID IT, HOORAY!

Congratulations! You've started *writing your movie*. It exists.

I suggest you don't read it. I suggest you lavish yourself in love or ice cream; however, you might need to read it—go ahead—but don't change anything and don't judge it. Just read it to get crazy about yourself.

Now go let visions of sugar plums dance in your head. We'll talk about it tomorrow.

You probably have a ton of questions from Day 1.

It's okay, they are the same ton everybody has. What we'll do is give you the answers you need at the moment. The other questions will answer themselves as we go:

### WRITERS ASK

*Q:* What if I go over ten pages?

*A:* That's okay. Somewhere in the last three pages will be a page-10 declaration; that is, you will have stated what the hero is going to pursue.

*Q:* What do I do with exposition? I've got to explain some things. I can't show it all.

*A:* Look to see if you have the character walk in and say, "Well, here we are in Paris because we won that vacation because I was top salesman."

Show not tell. Ask yourself, "Can I show this? How can I show this?"

Action/adventure movies often start with incredible hijinx, then cut to the office scene, where the plans are laid out. (Remember *Raiders of the Lost Ark?* Action, then the classroom. James Bond? Action, then the London office). If your characters need to lay out the plan, that's fine, but be forthright about it and actually call a meeting. Preferably after an action scene.

*Q:* How can I tell my story without revealing too much right away?

*A:* Reveal as much as you know as soon as you know it. Don't keep secrets from us. Don't hold back and don't try and trick your audience. You'll lose them. Too much too soon can be fixed, but too little too late rarely works.

When the audience comes to see your movie, you enter into an agreement with them. They are willing to accept the world you present to them if you agree to make it clear what they're supposed to understand about that world.

*Q:* Mine's a love story. It's about two people, not one, how do I tell both their stories?

*A:* The story can be about a twosome or three or a gang, but it is conveyed through one person. *Gone With the Wind* was a huge epic that told many people's stories and, in fact, it set out to be the story of the entire South, but it was conveyed through one person, Scarlett O'Hara. So ask yourself, "Whose story is this?" Whose point of view (P.O.V.) is the story told through?

*Q:* I've got lots of action. My main character is off the plane and in the cab and on the freeway and arrives home as the main credits finish. But when he opens the door I can't get him to talk.

*A:* There's a difference between action and movement. It's fine to show movement if it means something to your story. Is it building toward the story? Does it give information? If you have the character just spin his wheels because he can't get on with the story, create a device for yourself to get him to sit in a chair and deal with what he needs and wants.

*Q:* I'm writing a mystery. How do I plan the clues?
*A:* Answer this: Are you personality type X or type Y?

Do you make lists, make plans, and enjoy knowing the events of the day before you get to them? Then you are type X. Get a stack of 3x5 cards in colors. Decide what event leads to which suspect. Write the crime on the first card, and write the ending you want on the last card. Fill in between with cards giving clues that lead from the crime to the payoff. Use different color cards to track each path of the labyrinth you want to send us into. Then work out the 9-Minute structure of your story and drop in the clue cards along the way. In a mystery, the story tends to turn on events of the crime. If it is turning on a relationship or the growth of a character, ask yourself, "Do I really want to tell a mystery or is there a relationship story here that's more important to me?" If you want to tell a mystery, then just stick to the facts that cover or uncover the crime.

If you are personality type Y, you probably enjoy reading mysteries and want to write this one to find out "who done it" along with your audience. So don't have a plan; just have a crime and a strong crime solver. Do most of your story preparation fleshing out the character of your investigator, then have confidence that he will solve the mystery for you. Now start with a "what if." Show us a dead body. Have a vague idea how you'd like the payoff to come. Have a surprising, outrageous conclusion and see if you can write your way from crime to payoff by just stumbling on clues as they appear on the page. You will write the first draft very fast—as fast as it takes to read a good mystery.

Since you are solving this as you go, some of the leads you follow will be dead ends. Do this: when you read through, before rewrite, notice that you will have three variations of the same clue. Let's call them good, better, and best. Take elements from each and make the best one even more powerful and eliminate the other two. Keep building suspense and jeopardy. Scare yourself. Have your character dare to try the cellar door. If you can sustain your own excitement, you will sustain it for the audience as well.

### ENOUGH TALK—ACTION SPEAKS LOUDER THAN WORDS

Let's move on to Day 2 by reading Day 1.

This is how to read your speed pages from Day 1:

No judgments. You are allowed to ask yourself any questions except "Is it good?" or "Is it bad?"

Answer these questions:

- What's the story?
- Who is it about?
- What does the hero need?
- What does the hero want?
- Does it tell the story I wanted to tell?

Somewhere in yesterday's pages, did you tell us who and did you tell us what?

Can you restate the logline here?

(If you can do all that, great. Skip the next section. Go right to new pages.)

If you can't answer these questions, if you are depressed, overwhelmed, and/or confused, it's okay. Don't go back. Even though you feel you "should" go back to Day 1 and start again, don't go back. Always go forward. That's what the random draft is for, to find out what the movie is about. Keep moving forward.

Now. How do you do that when you don't know the story or the logline or anything? Remember your eight-minute exercise on what your story is about? Re-read it. Then *write for eight minutes* again.

▶▶▶▶▶▶▶▶▶▶▶▶▶▶▶▶▶▶▶▶▶▶▶▶▶▶▶▶▶▶▶▶▶▶▶▶▶▶▶▶

Underline what jumps out at you. There will be a three-word phrase that crystallizes what your movie is about. Look at your visual aid. Rekindle your initial feeling of what the story is saying. Remember, you're writing the random draft to find out what your movie is about. You now know more than you did before you started. The next twenty pages will reveal even more.

### HOW THE FIRST 10 PAGES LEAD TO THE NEXT 20

We already know a huge amount from your first ten pages. Whatever world you have set up you now build upon. Remember where you need to get to by page 30. That is where an event will happen that forces your hero to react.

We know *what* the story is about and we know *who* the story is about; now what other elements do you need to introduce to us in order to further your story along?

Act I is the place to set up everything you want us to know. Each scene should show character, advance the story, give information, build the situation, and express the viewpoint that you want us to understand.

Have you introduced us to the characters? What do we know about them so far?

What information have we gotten?

Notice the dialogue on the bottom of page 3. Does it tell you your attitude about doing this draft? Can you connect this attitude to a central question in your life that will tell you more about the story?

Now how do you get your hero from where he is on page 10 to where he needs to be on page 30? Stay with him.

Each scene advances the story and tells us something we don't already know. We're finding out more about this person, his world, his point of view, his problem. What does he want? What does he need? What are the obstacles? What else needs to be set up before page 30? Who else do we need to be introduced to?

If you feel yourself getting lost, it's because the main character is offstage. Bring him back to the center of action. Stay with him.

Turn on your inner projector. Let's do an exercise to bring your brain to the alpha state. Look at your visual aid, then close your eyes and roll them upward until your eyelids flicker. Picture your movie playing. Intensify the colors and the images. When you are ready, open your eyes and go.

Write for three hours. Follow your hero to the Act I event on page 30.

Just as the first ten pages told you the next twenty, those first thirty pages will now tell you about the next thirty. You're going to be alright.

### READ THE FIRST 30 PAGES

Look at where your character came from. Look at where he's going. Have you told us everything we need to know up to this moment? Do we know the hero well enough to know how he is likely to act, so that when he grows we see that he is acting differently?

Do not be concerned if you think you haven't done this. You have done this. You just don't know it yet.

Now accept your first thirty pages. I mean it. *Accept them.* If you don't, you'll be a lot of trouble to yourself when we need you the most.

### YOUR TURNING POINT

Today you need to get from the Act I turning point to the first indication of growth. Something has happened. Your hero is now on a course toward what he wants or he is reacting to an action that has happened to him. On page 45 you'll have a symbolic scene showing how this action is starting to affect him. It's a kind of summation scene that tells us where we've come to and where we're going.

Has this ever happened to you? You think you have a plan —you're getting ready—and then the phone rings and the plan is changed. It takes you a minute to get your twelve-ton train of thought going on a different track. Depending on the size of the surprise, you can actually feel it in your body. Your molecules screech to a stop. Regroup and slowly labor off in the new direction. Think of a time this has happened for you. Now, that is the feeling that your hero is experiencing at the Act I turn.

Let's say that the hero is getting ready to go visit his grandmother in the hospital. He gets a call that his grandmother has just died. What does he do? Often people in this situation go to the hospital anyway. Somehow they need to see the empty bed.

They need to be told again. They need to carry on their activities and assimilate the news slowly.

Remember, you are in the business of showing external action that reveals your character's inner feeling.

So—something has just happened to your character. What's he going to do now? Here are some choices human beings make. When we are stopped, when there is a sudden jolting change in our circumstances, we deny it, we get angry, we try to get back how it was. Finally, when we are ready, we accept it, and in the accepting we can go forward.

So that is page 30 to page 45. Jolt, then reaction. When we react in an old way to a new event, we get conflict. We are forced to react in a new way, and until we do, we will have conflict. Show us that conflict.

Here's an example from life: I have a friend whose husband left her. After some time of feeling devastated, she asked me to come and help move out his things. We were at this all afternoon, and it was not particularly difficult for her. Something was up. When we had emptied the closets and filled all the boxes, she said, "That's it, thanks." I wasn't about to leave—this was it, we were on the brink of something. She could have called anybody to help fill boxes. I knew she called me for something more.

We looked eye to eye—it was the moment of truth. It was a turning point. She ran into the bedroom and tore the sheets off the bed and fell into them crying.

And then I found out. Although she is normally a fastidious person and it had been several months since her husband left, she had not changed the sheets. They were her last intimate link with him. And now she was willing to accept that he was gone.

It was her page 45. A point of growth. He left at page 30; she spent fifteen pages in denial, anger, and despair, and now she was ready for acceptance.

Find that moment for your character. Don't stop short; don't stop at emptying closets and filling boxes. Find the outer action that illustrates symbolically the inner growth. Let's see a human being change.

Okay, that's all your head needs to know about it.

Take a deep breath. Write what's playing on pages 30–45.

Let's see your character grow.

## NO SAFETY IN PLAYING IT SAFE

                    INNER MOVIE
How are you?

                    YOU
Fine.

                    INNER MOVIE
But how are you really? Was it hard to
get here today?

Do you maybe feel this way?

Yesterday was great. You reached page 45 and a symbolic initial growth scene for your character. But today, something in you feels like a brick wall. And yet you showed up.

Now what.

That's exactly what happens for your character from pages 45 to 60. It's a time when you begin to see change take place.

Do you know someone who is overweight, goes on a diet, has initial success, loses weight, and almost immediately eats a dozen Ding-Dongs?

Here's a human trait: change scares us. *Inner Movie Axiom: We will do anything to change until we start to; then we do everything to stop it.*

Pages 45 to 60 is when your hero has put one foot in the boat but the other foot is still on the pier. You play him from 45 to 60 as wanting to get the other foot off the pier and into the boat so he can go.

On page 45 your character had initial success with his plans and has shown growth. Now the stakes get higher. As you know, when you first start something, there's a certain naivete. You have no idea what you're in for. You need this initial enthusiasm to start up. Your hero has stated his goal, has acted on it, has grown somewhat from it, and is a little bit different because of this. He needs to be a little bit different, because now he is faced with how difficult this is really going to be. If he had known initially that it was going to be this difficult, he might not have been able to handle it. So this slightly new person is more equipped to go after the dream.

Now how does that break down for your pages 45 to 60?

On page 45 is our first indication that the character takes action. Up until now he has been reacting to a situation. Once he starts taking action the obstacles no longer victimize him but rather challenge him. Where before the obstacles made him weaker, now they make him stronger. Let's see how he learns from the problem and takes new action.

Think in terms of cause and effect. One scene's cause is the next scene's effect, which in turn causes the next effect. For instance, in *Tootsie*, the agent tells Michael no one will hire him. In the next scene we see Michael as Dorothy on his/her way to an audition. The one scene caused the next. Can you see how each of your scenes becomes a natural progression from the scene before? Does one pull the next one along? Separately they don't necessarily make sense, but connected one to the other they make a complete story. And progression is just that —moving along. Your character is just a little more defined as we go.

### HOW TO CHANGE BEHAVIOR

We are watching your character experience obstacles so that he can learn new tools to use in each new scene.

Between pages 45 and 60, the obstacles heighten, they get tougher. But as the obstacles get tougher, the hero gets smarter, so that he is ready for each new obstacle.

He sees it's going to take everything he has to do this. It's harder than he thought, but somehow the fact that it is harder makes him want it more. Where before it was a wish, he senses the reality of accomplishment; there is light at the end of the tunnel.

It's harder, but he's learned something from what's happened up to now, two things in fact: (a) he's outgrown his previous life, so he can't go back; and (b) the goal seems closer, and he has gotten a few successes along that path. There's nothing more exhilarating for your hero than to be spurred on by a few small successes.

Here's how it will work in your pages. Page 45 is the symbolic growth scene. It is a taste of where your hero will get to. Page 60 is where he commits wholeheartedly to his dream. In *Gone With the Wind* Scarlett holds the carrots up to the sky and says, "As God is my witness, I'll never go hungry again." And she spends the second half of the movie holding to that commitment.

### I HAVE MET THE ENEMY AND IT IS ME

By page 60 your character is going to be saying loud and clear what he began to state as a dream on page 3.

Have your character complete this statement now: "As God is my witness, I will —— —— ——."

### IT'S WHAT IT IS; IT'S NOT WHAT IT ISN'T

If you'll notice, you might be experiencing this for yourself. Any illusion you had about what you thought it was like to write a movie is going through changes now. The illusion is giving way to reality, and in reality is where real progress is made.

Any obstacles that you are now experiencing come from the discrepancy between what you thought you were supposed to experience and what you really are experiencing. The way to eliminate discrepancy is to just have one experience at a time. So give up how you thought it was going to be. That way you can *enjoy* how it is.

Okay. Let's go. Pages 45 to 60. Let's see your hero move from initial growth on page 45 to strong commitment on page 60. Let's see him get better and better at surmounting obstacles.

Okay, you are committed. Your character has stated, "As God is my witness, I will —— —— ——." This is where your character declares his belief and stands by it.

Nothing is going to stop him now. If you want him to prove himself, this is where he does it. This is his time to be tested, and he's passing with straight A's, even though the obstacles get very hard.

As he gives up where he was in order to get where he wants to go, he finds himself in midair. The only thing that sustains you when you're in midair is your belief. Without it you'd fall on your face. But he's got faith now, and he's got tools. You've been making him stronger and stronger from pages 45 to 60.

In the first half of Act II, we saw stakes of obstacle. Now show us stakes of issue.

### WHAT ARE STAKES OF OBSTACLE/STAKES OF ISSUE?

For the first half of Act II, (pages 30 to 60), your hero is saying, "I want it. I want it." And the stakes against him are obstacles that seem to say, "you can't have it."

Then on page 60 your hero says, "I am going to have it!" He's saying obstacles don't matter, he'll just knock them over. He's committed.

Now what he wants starts to change from a dream to a reality, and *when your dream changes to reality is when you get realistic about your dream.*

Stakes of issue are questions like "Do I really want it?" "Am I willing to give up this to have that?" "Now that I'm standing on the precipice looking at this thing, is it worth it because I've really been through it already and I see it but I'm not there yet?" Do you see how he's now dealing with his dream realistically and the stakes are ones of issue? In asking himself these questions he is now willing to change.

### ALMOST ANSWERED PRAYERS

In *The African Queen*, Katharine Hepburn and Humphrey Bogart have been through it all. This is it; this is the end; they are in a bog. They've tried every which way to get out and now they fall in an exhausted embrace of deep sleep. The camera pulls out and we see that they are three feet from the open sea.

### THE PERFECT EVENT

We need to quit when we are three feet from the open sea. Because then an event happens. In the case of *The African Queen*, it starts to rain.

Before page 75 there is a scene where your hero will just about give up what he committed to on page 60. (This example from *The African Queen* actually occurs later than page 75, but since it's such a strong cinematic image, we'll use it anyway.)

### HE HAS TO LET IT GO

There comes a moment when the thing wanted becomes the thing gotten. That moment turns on a very important change in attitude.

*Inner Movie Axiom: In order to have a dream become a reality, it must be given up as a dream.* Then it happens. How? Because of the event that occurs. In *African Queen*, the key change came when they were willing to fall into a deep sleep with each other. The exhaustion of fighting for their goal brought the greater goal into focus. They gave up. That way they gave the event *a chance to occur* and make the dream a reality.

### DO WHAT YOU DO AND IT WORKS

You can work and work on something and try to force a space for it where there wasn't one. But no matter what heroics you perform, it needs something else. That something else is— you need to let it go. Trust that you've done everything you can do. Now let what you sent out come back.

I have a friend who was on the phone constantly, generating business. She called me to bemoan the fact that nobody had returned her calls. It was because she was still on the phone! Stop generating, let the world come to you.

Okay, pages 60 through 75. To learn is to let yourself enter new territory. Do everything you can, then let it go.

Take two hours now. See where your hero takes you—even to places you had no idea you'd go. ▶▶▶▶▶▶▶▶▶▶▶▶▶▶▶▶▶▶▶▶▶▶▶▶▶▶

(Please read today's first section in the early A.M.)

Hi. You're mad today. You didn't want to show up. You think this book is ——(fill in the blank). You want to strangle it and throw it across the room. You are frustrated, confused, and *you want to give up!*

Fantastic! That's the assignment for today—give up.

Live all day empty, with no thought of your movie. Every time your mind lands on your movie, repeat this *Inner Movie Axiom: If you go where you don't know to go, you'll get there.* (If this doesn't make sense to you, good. It is meant to be a brain twister. Because up until now you have been concentrating on solving your character's central problem. Now your brain needs to switch from the problem mode to the solution mode. So go now, and let your brain "twist.") ▬▬▬▬▬▬▬▬▬▬▬▬▬

### LATER—PROBLEM SOLVING 101

If you have a problem, state the problem. Simple. But here's why you still have the problem: you haven't stated the problem; you stated the solution. And the solution that you've stated is not correct.

*Inner Movie Axiom: If you state the solution you still have the problem. If you state the problem, you are free to solve it.*

Here's an example:

You need to find a ladder to reach the ceiling. You can't find a ladder, therefore you can't reach the ceiling.

The ladder is the false solution to reaching the ceiling, the false problem.

The problem is the bulb burned out.

Now list ten activities relating to a burned-out bulb that do not include a ladder.

In our never-ending quest to look for the most efficient way to do something, we often miss the *best* way to do it.

Now you may ask, "What does this problem solving stuff have to do with Day 6?" I'm glad you asked. Up until now your hero has been after a solution to his problem. He stated the solution he was looking for and he looked for it.

But, he didn't find his solution.
*Something found him.*

*Inner Movie Axiom: Go ahead and look for something, but* it *will find* you.

### NOW TO YOUR PAGES 75–90

Once the page-75 event occurs, it's the hero's chance to seize this event as an opportunity. If this event had happened in the beginning of your movie, it would have destroyed him, but now he is changed, and the changed way he thinks is expressed through new behavior. This event has occurred to give him the opportunity to strut his new stuff. If he doesn't strut his stuff, the event can destroy him. So therefore the event forces him to be stronger.

From pages 75 to 90 you'll move very fast. Your hero got up the mountain, and now he's shooting the rapids on the other side. There is no stopping him and no stopping the events around him. He has everything to do to keep up with and be on top of events. He is not fighting blockage here; he is commanding flow. He is getting his life to change now. And yet this wasn't what he thought would happen. This wasn't what he expected.

For instance, he didn't expect that he would find a heroine and that she would be helping. And that without her help it all wouldn't be happening. He went up the mountain to find himself, he came down the mountain with her. He found her because he *did* find himself, and she then became his gift for achieving what he planned. If he went up to find her, he would probably come down having found himself.

Do you see how this is the point in the script when you get to get more than you planned for?

This time through on the random draft, you might not be completely satisfied with your pages 75 to 90. That is because you are still pushing toward the solution you thought would work. Let it go. Be willing to let your character stumble around. The solution will find him.

Go ahead. Write 75 to 90. Write it very fast. Steamroll through plenty of action. Let it all surprise you. Get it down in as short and fast a time as you can.

Go ahead. Watch your character grow. ∞∞∞∞∞∞∞∞∞∞∞∞∞∞∞∞∞∞

> INNER MOVIE
> Guess what? You're going to write
> thirty pages today.

> YOU
> Thirty pages. Oh no!

This will probably be the easiest day so far. You are not allowed to write for more than three hours.

Here's what goes on these thirty pages:

You need to take us from crisis to ending. We need to have all loose ends tied up. Everything that got started gets finished now. You will be carrying out the resolution of the story. Answer these questions:

- Does your hero get what he wanted?
- What last thing does he have to give up to get it?
- How is he different in the end than he was in the beginning?

Remember your first scene of the movie—see if the last scene can be an answer to that scene. We call this bookends. Say the first scene is of two young people in wartime who get married on the refugee truck during a barrage of gunfire. The movie is the story of their lives together and the last scene is their fiftieth wedding anniversary celebration, where they finally have a traditional wedding ceremony. See if you can find a bookend scene. Jot it down on a 3 x 5 card. Now work backward.

Make a list of the points that you need to settle in order to resolve all the action, and write each down on a 3 x 5 card. Do not formulate the scenes, just write a note (e.g., "needs to rescue horse, finds out rancher was shot"). When you have cards for all the loose ends, put them in the order in which the action will appear, beginning with the first event and ending with your bookend scene. Remember, Act III is the resolution. This is where the problems get solved. Work very quickly.

Now run Act III on your inner projector. There will be very detailed, heartfelt scenes and there will be gaping holes. That's as it should be at this point. You'll need those gaping holes to move around in when you rewrite.

Okay. This is it. The finale. The Big Payoff. Everything you picked up and ran with, you now put down in a new light.

Remember the good feeling you get when you watch a movie and it starts to pay off at the end? It's exciting; when the Raiders finally found the lost ark and looked inside; when Humphrey Bogart and Ingrid Bergman are finally at the airport in *Casablanca*. Be dramatic here. Give us some beautiful closing moments.

Ready begin . . . .

## THE END

You did it! It's done! You're amazing! Celebrate immediately.

There's nothing more you have to do today.

Congratulations! Hooray, you have a random draft. Be very, very happy. Go ahead, let yourself off.

This is a day of rest. But that doesn't mean you don't have an assignment.

How you rest affects the entire outcome of your script.

Here's your assignment.

Do you feel that your random draft is doggie do? If so, then *change your mind*; tomorrow you can change your pages. What we want from you today is unbridled, unabashed, mad, abandoned joy with yourself for being a screenwriter and having written a screenplay. Let people congratulate you. Let them take you to dinner. Give yourself a party. Pet the dog.

Be particularly kind to yourself physically. Administer favorite foods. Fall asleep on the couch.

Because if you don't reward your body, then you can't ask it to do hard work through the rewrite. You'll have a fight on your hands later that you won't be able to win. So reward yourself lavishly and your body will be happy to cooperate, because it will know there will be more rewards after the next stint of work.

My body actually has me trained:

> BODY
> Let me get this straight...you worked
> us 'til dawn and you want to do the
> same tonight? Oh no, honey child, not
> until we shop.

So your assignment is to be very good to yourself. But that's not all.

Curiously, of all the 21 Days that we take to write your script, this is the one day that you might need to expand, because there are several changes in yourself you have to experience before you begin to rewrite.

First, you need to detach from the script. Up until now you have had to hold to a leap of faith that you could do this. You pulled a thought out of thin air and made nothing into something. It was in you; now it's on the table. It has a life of it's own. I like a quote from Joyce Maynard on birth at home: "In a house where there had been three people, there were now four, although no one had come in the door."

What we are after is a shift in perception. You need to value the birth of your script. It exists. Now all it needs is developing. You want to understand that so you don't go giving birth to it again. You have completed the beginning. You are beyond the beginning. All you have to do now is finish it.

You need to detach in another way. The part of you that jumped and romped and brainstormed all over the page was given free rein; you were encouraged to write from your heart. Now we are going to rewrite from your head. Where before we asked "what if" to broaden and open, now we'll ask "what if" to clarify and define.

Notice that you have created a constant all week through the random draft. Either you've worn the same type of shirt or eaten just chili. See if you can identify the constant. It's an important tool your subconscious uses. If you can't unearth it, then look to a ritual that you do each day before writing. What we want now is for you to add something to this constant, something that will alert your head, that you're continuing on but that your head is now invited to put its two "sense" in.

Here's an example from my life. I started a script one morning while wearing my baseball cap. So every morning of the random draft I wore my baseball cap. When I switched to rewrite, I switched to my vintner's hat. (I got an added bonus in this plan. Since a vintner's hat is the kind worn at a winery, I naturally had a bottle of champagne when the script was done.)

If you try, you can be just as eccentric. So find your constant now and add a helpful detail.

There is one last task. When you first look up from the random draft, after seven days, you might experience the sensation of parallax; a kind of blurry-eyed slow motion view. *Your world has changed* but everybody else is going on as usual. Don't they know?! Can't they see?! You will want to change them. Here's what to do instead, change one small thing in yourself. We're still after perception shift here. Notice the wisdom you've acquired as a result of completing the random draft.

Find a new way that you belong in the world, based on your

central question you are exploring in your script. How are you relating to people differently? What situations can you rethink? What has the random draft taught you about want and need?

Answer all that and we'll see you tomorrow for the read through.

## DAY 9: THE GOOD, THE BAD, THE UGLY; READING THE RANDOM DRAFT

Here's what you are *not* going to do today:

You are not going to judge your script. You are not going to ask, "Am I a writer?" You are not going to cry.

A word about good and bad. Your script isn't either of these and it's always both. You are not allowed to ask, "Is it good? Is it bad?" You are going to ask only these questions:

- Does this scene work?
- What did I want to show here?
- Can I show it another way more effectively?

What you have is a work in progress. This day in the process is to see what's there and to begin to see what needs to be added.

If you judge the script now, what you are doing is judging yourself. You are a writer because you wrote the random draft. What kind of a writer you are can't be determined until after the rewrite.

The best way to assure that in the end you will be pleased with yourself as a writer is to not worry about that now, in the middle.

We need you detached from any questions of self-worth, because all your concerns now have to be with working out the script.

You've given birth. Now let's see who this kid is. Switch from anticipation to participation. Let it take on a life of its own.

Okay. Read your random draft. Out loud. Quickly. In one sitting. All the way through. Don't skip scenes because you can't bear to look at them or because you think the scene is perfect. Read it all equally. You may dash down a few short notes, but this is *reading* day, not *rewriting* day.

So read.

wwwwwwwwwwwwwwwwwwwwwwwwwwwwwwwwwwwwwwwwww

### NOW WHAT?

Quite an experience, isn't it—reading all the way through it?

In spite of what we said about judging, you did it anyway.

You know how you are. You thought some things were there and they aren't. You were worried about other spots that actually played beautifully.

It's different than you thought, isn't it? Now, look immediately to your visual aid. Rekindle the original concept and then merge what you thought it was with how it is.

Ask this of yourself:

- Is the story that I wanted to tell the story I told?
- Is it true to my original feeling?

The act of writing the script might have caused you to explore your central question to such an extent that you answered the question. Answering a theme often changes the theme.

Let's say you set off to prove that the world is evil and everybody's in danger. But something happened in the script when your character was combatting evil. You were finding that evil was within him. Now your theme becomes "The world is how you create it for yourself."

The task for you right now is to hold to your original vision, yet allow what you learned when you explored that vision to change the vision.

Which leads us back to the logline:

- Is it still the movie you want to write?
- Is it the movie you have written?

Tomorrow after an overview we'll zoom in on each page. Right now look at the big picture. In fact—let's say you just saw this up on the big screen and now someone is asking what kind of theater experience you just had.

- Did you know what it was about?
- Could you identify with the characters?
- Was this movie about what you thought it was about?

Now lie down on the floor. Let it hold you. Rest your bones. Is your neck stiff? Let it all go. You're finished writing. All you have to do now is rewrite.

# YOUR REWRITE DRAFT;
# REWRITE FROM YOUR HEAD

## DAY 10: REWRITE ACT I; PAGES 1–10

You're going to love this. It's the easy part. You get to be smart, even analytical, if you must. You get to use your good old tried and true best business brain. I hope you're happy.

### BEYOND THE RANDOM DRAFT

If you've been aching to say stuff like "dramatic momentum," "plot continuity," or "plausible motivation," today is your day.

Let's talk about *your* script.

I realize I haven't read it yet, but we won't let that stop us.

Since we're not in the same room at the moment, I need to ask you a few things so we can get a clear fix on what your script needs for rewrite.

### WHO ARE YOU?

Are you brain smart? Do you lead with your head? Do you read the newspapers voraciously? Do world issues concern you? When you have dinner with a friend, are you more likely to talk about politics than your love life?

Let's call you Yang.

Are you intuitive? Do you lead with your heart? Do your perceptions of life come to you from personal observation?

When you have dinner with a friend, do you talk about everything? Do you remember the food?

Let's call you Yin.

*Yang:* Your script structure probably hinges on external events and actions. It's in the mystery, thriller, or crime-action-adventure genre. You have a strong hero, but we don't know much about him (like Clint or Duke).

*Yin:* Yours is probably an inner story. The character is on a journey of self-discovery. Themes are love and personal growth. It is intimate in scale and deep in scope.

*Yang:* Since you're good at structure, you are probably satisfied with that aspect of your script. But there's a flatness, a coldness to the story. You think you should put in more action. Go the other way. Every time it seems to go flat or slows down, zoom in on the hero and give us a quiet scene that shows more of him. The way to do this is to ask your character personal questions. Imagine you went to high school with him. Reminisce. Write out a page of conversation between the two of you. Conversation is different than dialogue. Chances are that in your script he's always got a smart line, like "Go ahead, make my day." So in the conversation that you write, let's see the feelings behind the smart lines. You don't have to use this conversation in your script; we just want him talking to you, so that at least *you* know him. That way you can tell us. Of course, the best way is for the character to show us his feelings directly.

*Yin:* You probably love your character. You know you have lots of great scenes, but you can't really say what they are about. You're not sure if there's really a story. Your script is long. Act I, you think, goes to at least page 45, perhaps even page 60—you're not sure.

I'm going to say the most terrible word to you. I hope you're sitting down. Here's what you're going to have to do. Cut.

In any script there are *x* number of scenes you actually need to move the story along. In your script you have at least three variations of each of those scenes. Do this: read each scene. Ask, "What does this scene do to move the story along?" Find which other scenes serve the same purpose. Put them together. Now see how you can incorporate all *like* scenes into one *bril-*

*liant* scene that tells the jokes, shows the character, proves your talent but most importantly, *moves the story along*. You will have to make up a batch of what I call ego stew—which is a stock pot into which you throw great jokes and brilliant pieces of writing that don't fit into the script. I realize this talk is causing you heart palpitations. However, you and the script will be fine as soon as you're willing to accept that true brilliance is simplicity, not complication. If you insist on keeping in all your hero's lovable antics, then we will not love him, we will want to throw tomatoes.

### LET'S GET MORE PERSONAL

Do you feel this way in your life right now: you want to get going? You want to climb out of a hole you've been in and make changes in your life? Then on the first few pages your character will be moving into a new apartment, or quitting his job, or in some way going from dormancy to movement. This first spurt of action from your character is *the result* he wishes. This is an important element of structure. We'll need to know why you chose to start the story at this moment.

### WHY YOU STARTED WHERE YOU STARTED

Does your hero start out with action but immediately bogs down? Was the central question never really clear to you? Did you change the central question many times? Then you might have had big trouble with page 30.

From page 1 to page 3, you managed to get the character going; however, he stops by page 10, because though he has left where he was, he doesn't know where to go. Your script then goes back and plays his past. You might even have flashbacks. But here's the flash: The story you're telling is backstory—the character's history. He's still there; he isn't yet *here*. You are telling us where the character has *been*, not yet where he's going.

### HOW DO I GET HERE FROM THERE?

Picture the whole first act. Did you throw your hero out into the world on page 1 and then find him pounding on the door to get back in by page 10? Is he somehow missing or asleep from pages 10 through 30? Look at metaphors. Is he dragging around excess baggage? Has his watch stopped? Look at the dialogue. Are minor characters saying, "Where's Marty?"

Here are two symptoms:

1. Did you get to page 30 in your random draft and come to a stone cold stop?
2. Do you have everything you know about your hero in the first 30 pages but nothing seems to be happening until page 30?

Here's relief:

Your page 30 is actually where your movie starts. Look at it now; see if this allows Act II to suddenly come alive.

Does this realization make you feel free? Kind of like a chiropractor popping your spine back in alignment. Great.

Now what are you going to do with pages 1 to 30? Keep them. Just add page-3 and page-10 declarations that move us forward in the story. Notice what backstory scenes you don't need and get rid of them. That way you're free to move the story forward.

Okay, that's enough of The Big Picture for today.

## ZOOM IN

Let's rewrite pages 1 through 10.

This is the day you're going to switch modes. You are going from heart to head.

Where up until now we've dashed down pages, now we're going to fill in holes.

Read your pages 1 to 10 again.

Here's your page 1.

There's a metaphor on this page. It will give you a *huge* clue as to what your story wants to be about.

Here are some examples:

- A stallion running wild; cut to main character in prison. This story is about freedom.
- A main character trips over his own feet. The story is of him learning to get out of his own way.
- A car won't start. This is the story of how your character gets from stop to go.

Find the metaphor. What did you tell yourself on page 1?

See how brilliant you are when you're not trying? Take a moment now to see how the initial metaphor tells thematically your whole story.

Your "rewrite part" needs to respect your "write part" for coming up with the perfect metaphors.

It's your job to understand what the metaphors mean.

The random draft is similar to a dream. You think some image is weird until suddenly it makes sense.

If you have a weird image sticking out that doesn't belong, ask yourself why it's there. Here's what it isn't: It isn't wrong. *Inner Movie Axiom: It only feels wrong if you don't know why it's right*.

### PAGE 1

Notice the scene you chose here. Does it give us backstory (e.g., a young girl in wedding dress fleeing the wedding on a motorcycle)? In other words, do we have a sense that someone already lives and we're just joining them at this moment? Have you given us a sense of place, time, tone? If it's a comedy, is there a joke yet? Do we know something about the flavor of the world you are presenting? Do we see character?

### WHAT TO LOOK FOR

Is your first page very tight with detail, every nuance captured, no gesture left to chance? Did you work and hone and perfect this? Are you now quite proud of it? Look at it now. You have camera angles and more than three details to introduce each person and place. Is your first page mostly description? Free yourself from this right away. See where you can replace tight details with just three choice words.

Give us a general picture. Let's get the mood and atmosphere. Yes, *do* choose the details that are going to give the audience information, but hone down. Coco Chanel said, "Get dressed—just before you walk out the door, take off one piece of jewelry." It's the one piece too many that you don't need. See what detail you can eliminate now.

NOTE: What you're writing here is a script to be read. Before it's a shooting script it's a reading script. Get the *reader* interested—paint word pictures. (It is a known fact that 80 percent of producers only read 20 percent of the description.)

If you are visually imaginative or action-oriented, you probably have great sweeping movement—out of the plane, through the airport, into the limo, onto the turnpike. Fine. What's happening? There is a difference between movement and action. If nothing is revealed about the character or the story or the mood or the atmosphere, all that visual "noise" doesn't amount to anything. Replace movement with action.

### PACING

Remember, each page is one minute. Look at your room for one minute. One minute is a very long time. Our eye takes in an enormous amount of information very quickly. Move through visuals fast. A picture is worth a thousand words. Show us the pictures.

List everything we know by the bottom of page 1—it better be a lot. At least ten concrete facts showing point of view, place, character, arena, time, mood.

### HOW TO STATE YOUR CENTRAL QUESTION

Your character does not have to get up on a podium and state the central question. For instance a battered housewife needn't say "my husband has beat me for seven years and I have to get away because the most important thing I want is freedom." Show don't tell. Here's an example:

INT. RANSACKED APARTMENT - NIGHT

Husband exits. Slams door. KAY, trembling, looks at the reflection of her swollen eye in goldfish bowl.

> KAY
> (to fish)
> At least you're free.

This line of dialogue does a couple of things. It gives us story, what situation Kay's in. It also shows how she feels about her situation, how she's handling it, what her character is; and mainly it foreshadows that she wants freedom. Here's a woman so desperate for communication she's talking to a goldfish.

Did you say something on page 3 and something on page 10 that tells us who your story's about and what it's about?

Here's an example:

> If I don't get those
> guys, I'll never be able to show my
> face around here again.

### WHAT IS A SCENE AND HOW DO I MAKE MINE WONDERFUL?

Enter a scene at the last best moment. A scene does not need a beginning, middle, and end; it needs to take care of business and be done.

Ask yourself what this scene needs to show. You can even make a list. Then let your imagination do the work of coming up with the best way to show these things. It does not have to be one scene. It could be a series of quick cuts.

Once you've shown what you need to show, get out.

You don't have to end the action. There's another scene right behind this that keeps it going. Get out as soon as you show us what we need to see. Think in cause and effect, cause and effect. This scene causes the next one. The next scene is the effect of the previous one.

Answer these questions about each of your scenes.

- What is the purpose of this scene?
- Is this the best possible way to convey that purpose?
- Do I need this scene? Does it advance the story? Did I already express the information? Does this scene build from the one before? Did the scene before *cause* this scene? Is this scene the *effect* of the scene before it?
- Is my story building? Does the audience know a little more?
- Is my hero different now than in previous scenes?
- Do I know where he came from; where he is going?
- Do the scenes reflect how I wanted the story to progress?
- Does my hero stop action by saying, "We'll talk about this in the morning."?
- Do I drop the dramatic ball by letting too much time pass between action and expression of emotion?

• Do I stop one action and invent another? Do I let action build by stacking events layer upon layer?

## WRITERS ASK

*Q:* What can I do? My dialogue seems flat.

*A:* We hope that up until now you have been conjuring your scenes from real life, not from remembered movies, in other words, from what *you* would say if someone had a gun to your head, rather than from what have you heard said in a thousand such scenes in a thousand previous movies.

Look at your dialogue. Is it revealing enough about your characters and their relationships, or is it just "Hi, Joe." "Hi." "This is Sarah." "Nice to meet you."

*Q:* I have lots of description, but nothing's happening. How can I create more action?

*A:* You're controlling action by making the description too detailed.

Don't tell us what we can't see in the description. Do your characters talk rather than take action? Read one of these "talking heads" scenes. Now decide what the scene is supposed to convey and do that in a single action and no dialogue. Do that now.

*Q:* How come my story seems fake when it's based on a real-life occurrence?

*A:* You're just not telling the whole truth yet. If you have a real story but you tell fake parts, those are the parts we won't like and will know are false.

Tell your truth and it will be true for others. If it's not true for others, you just haven't told the *whole* truth yet. Stop keeping secrets and it will have value.

So that's plenty enough to get you through the first ten pages. Just concentrate on those today. We are off the whole picture and onto each page.

## WHAT TO DO TODAY

If you haven't switched from the overview to the specific, then go for a walk before you rewrite pages 1 through 10. In the random draft, we were seeing the forest; now look at the trees.

Before you begin to rewrite, do two things to release your creativity: listen to music; and then take a deep breath, close your eyes, roll them up into your head, and feel your eyelids tweaking. Now you're in an alpha state. It's a particularly smart part of the brain.

Hold this thought: an artist takes us by the eye and leads us through his painting; he shows us what's dominant and what's subordinate. You now need to take us by the heart into the world you want us to experience.

Go now and rewrite pages 1 through 10. ~~~~~~~~~~~~~~~~~~~~~~~~

### HOW TO WRITE A MOVIE

Let's discuss some fundamental techniques of movie writing. You may wonder why we didn't mention all these before. The reason is, you probably handled these techniques naturally. You've seen so many movies in your lifetime, you are an expert after all. We'll just list them so you can use them in rewrite.

### EXPOSITION

Talk is cheap except in movies. In movies, too much talk costs you.

It is not the character's job to tell us the story. It's your job. You need to show, not tell. The artful way you chose this character, in this place, saying these lines, shows us far more than any of these elements alone.

This is the day you'll be dealing with exposition in your script. If at any time you stop action to give us information, look at how you do it. Are we seeing anything else in the scene? From page 10 to page 30 all your scenes should build one to the next, giving information about character and setting up the situation. The use of Act I is to set up all the new business. By page 30 we will have to be pretty much finished with new business. So handle it all here and reveal it to us by *show*, not tell.

### DIALOGUE IS NOT CONVERSATION

Let's take a line of dialogue, three words, and see how many stories it can tell. The line is, "Come on, Lou." Now, you be the actor. Say the line as it would be said in each of these situations: Lou is an old dog, a puppy, the lead horse running the Kentucky Derby on which you've bet your life savings. Lou is a man, a woman, a boy, a girl, a human who wants to leave with aliens, a prizefighter on the mat, a prostitute, a crash victim dying in his friend's arms.

Do you see that dialogue is a function of story? Three words can tell a whole story; all you have to do is choose their context. Look at your dialogue now. Where it doesn't say enough, choose again.

### THERE IS NO INTROSPECTION IN MOVIES

We can see what the characters do. We can hear what they say. We can't see or hear what they're thinking unless there's a voice-over narration (in which case we are told what they think). But guess what—that's just like real life. The only person you know introspectively is yourself. So how in life do you pick up what somebody else is thinking?

### HOW TO READ MINDS

Did anybody ever say to you, "*I AM NOT ANGRY!!!*"

Think of the ways in which you understood what was really being conveyed to you. What were the person's true needs and wants? How did you know that? List twenty ways you knew, without being told directly, what the person was really feeling.

### HOW TO READ DIALOGUE

Now that you are aware of at least twenty ways that character has been revealed to you, you can use those to reveal your characters. Just when we think nobody is listening, when we think we're talking about something else, we will tell the deepest truth about ourselves.

Here's an example: I was conducting a writer's workshop at a prison. There was one inmate who hadn't spoken all day. I said, "How do you feel about that, Gerald?" Suddenly it was as though the room gasped. I got the collective message "Don't mess with Gerald."

I asked him how he felt when he was alone in his cell at night trying to write his story. He thought he was telling about his writer's block. He described how it was choking him. He couldn't breathe. It stopped his blood. And yet the blood rushed. A glaze came over his eyes and he stood up and spoke in loud, disjointed words. He held his pencil in his fist and stabbed the air over and over again. I realized that he was describing the violent crime he had committed.

### THE SPLIT-SECOND STORY

Last Thanksgiving with the family, what happened? Everybody gathered together, ate, watched football, did the dishes. But what was *really* going on?

Find the split-second story now (e.g., Dad sneaks a drink, Mother pretends to not see, drops the cranberries on daughter's lap, daughter runs to her childhood room, sits in the rocker with her teddy bear of twenty years ago). *Show us where to look.*

## REVEAL CHARACTER IN SMALL DETAILS

You will find that you will keep secrets about your hero. The other characters will be much clearer because they are outside you, but the hero will be less clear. This is because these things are obvious to you. Go ahead and reveal them. Keep telling the truth.

## WRITERS ASK

*Q:* I have a farce and I have twelve main characters to set up. What am I going to do?

*A:* Farce is unique in that it is all very tightly setup to springboard into the first payoff in Act II. Think of yourself as an expert juggler in a funny costume. Do the setting up in sight gags. Since farce relies on a nonsequitor, you can setup several characters and situations in one visual scene. Look at your first twenty pages. You might have three variations on each scene. Combine action and eliminate two of the three scenes. Tighten. You'll have to have one-third the jokes and be three times as funny.

*Q:* All my characters talk too much. There's no action. But I don't think I'm telling the action instead of showing it. I just don't know what action to give them.

*A:* If everybody's uttering lofty concepts but can't move, it is probably an issue story. It's not about this man and this woman in this situation. Personalize it immediately. If they are talking at a restaurant and say, "People have no feelings, they're afraid to be intimate." *They are talking about themselves!* Throw them into action: Waiter spills flaming desert on Jackie. Jack grabs at Jackie to douse the flames. Her blouse disintegrates in his hands. Now let's see what they do with the intimacy.

If you find yourself writing lofty speeches, go back to portraying how your hero is affected by his world. It is not your function as movie writer to save the world. The world is fine. Just be willing to contribute your one clear note to the symphony of life. That's plenty enough.

### OKAY, LET'S REWRITE

Look at your pages 10 through 30. Are you showing us everything we need to know? Is the main character in most of the scenes? This is our chance to see what his problem is. What's his problem?

It's especially important for the scenes to build one to the next. Look at your scenes. If any are similar, combine them and move the story along. Notice the pace of the scenes. Are they quick? Do you get in, take care of needed business, and get out? Or do you unravel information slowly—a little about him, a little about her until they meet in the subway on page 30. Whatever the pace, is it building? Is it how you want it?

Here's the nature of pages 10 to 30:

Think of the process of how you meet someone and they become your friend.

You are introduced. You get an initial impression. You have an idea of what he's like. You talk briefly and find out a little about what he'd like for his life. You know very little about him. But you know at least one thing. you know you like him. That would be page 1 to 10 of a friendship.

Pages 10 to 30 could be your getting together and learning more about him. Friendships are often elusive in the beginning stages. You call each other; you can't seem to find common time. When you suggest you meet at his house, he might be abrupt and hang up, and you don't know why. Later, when you do get to know him and go to his house, you find he was embarrassed about it because it's a dump. You also find yourself changing your opinion about him based on the further information that you're getting. You were interested because you had questions about him. Now you're interested because of the answers.

So that's what Act I is—friendship. Let us get to know your character. Let us be his friend.  ▸▸▸▸▸▸▸▸▸▸▸▸▸▸▸▸▸▸▸▸▸▸▸▸▸▸▸▸▸▸▸▸▸▸

### DID YOU EVER DO THIS

You were excited about a trip. You had planned it for weeks. You knew it was going to be perfect, because you had imagined it down to the last detail.

The day comes. Your alarm doesn't go off. You wake up and dash out and forget your snow goggles, the ones you envisioned wearing at the top of the slope when the glory of the mountain was going to give you the answer to life. You finally get to the airport. The reservation is snafu. You get on the plane late, you get the middle seat, you start your joyous trip wanting to kill the fat man next to you.

Here's the problem:

*It's not the circumstances, it's the plan.* If you try to fit the square peg of circumstance into the round hole of what you had planned, all you get is frustrated. You have to *switch from anticipation to participation*:

Here's what you might find yourself doing today. Trying to make the story what you wanted it to be rather than seeing what it is. Instead, see what you've actually got and work from there. That way the whole story will go forward into what's new rather than backward into what's old.

Look at your main character. Is he living in anticipation instead of participation? Is he holding to his original plan but not taking any real actions to get going? Does he see what's really occurring around him, and is he integrating it into his plan?

### CONSIDER YOUR LOGLINE

Is what he wanted going to be what he gets? From the random draft you're beginning to see that there is something more to this story than you originally thought.

Did your logline express a belief that you are changing? If you've changed your mind, change the logline. It's okay. Adjust your logline to keep up with you.

The scene of initial growth that should appear around page 45 is a good clue as to where the story wants to go.

Let's talk a bit here about how you arrived at your story.

When you were first getting ready to write, did you have not one story but three? Did you go with one, then quickly commit to the other, then maybe a third one suddenly took over, and that's your story now?

Well, don't worry—they were all the same story. One might have taken place in the seventeenth century, and one might have been about toxic waste, but they were the same story. These seemingly different stories reflect your subconscious at work searching for the best metaphor (among many possible story ideas) to explore your current life issue. Think of a road map with various routes leading to the same destination. You have a choice, but the result is the same. *What* you write about remains constant, even though *how* you write about it may change.

Now, as you are reconsidering your logline, remember the other stories and see how they all wanted to tell the same story. Be clear on what that story is.

If one of your stories had a teenage hero and one had a forty-five-year-old hero, the stories could still be the same told from different sides of the same experience. Your subconscious seeks out your story and explores the range of ages in which the problem might be solved. The stories tend to be about where *you* have come from on a particular issue and where you want to go with it.

For instance, say that you are going through a divorce now at age thirty-eight, and you wonder what went wrong. You might have a story of a nineteen-year-old just getting married and one of a fifty-year-old just widowed.

You might want to explore your uncertainty about marriage in your future: "Should I trust marriage again, or should I try it alone?"

Both stories, the one of the nineteen-year-old and the one of the fifty-year-old, will answer your questions. As a general rule, if you are stuck, consider making the character your age exactly. It will clarify what's on your mind about the matter. It's great when a character tells you what you haven't been able to say.

*Q:* You might ask, "If the hero is me, why do I know all the other characters better than I know the hero?"

*A:* Don't you sometimes know everybody else better than you know yourself? It's a matter of perspective. It's easy to see other people's problems and what they should do.

It's very different for us to have that kind of clarity about ourselves. All you have to do is be sincere about not hiding. Keep telling the truth.

### ANCILLARY CHARACTERS ARE NOT PEOPLE

*All* the characters are *aspects* of you. If you have created a triangle, there is one main character. The other two are polar aspects of the main character. Maybe one represents what you want to leave. One represents what you want to get. When you view your characters as aspects of the main character, they won't take control or run you offtrack.

Let the main character take power back from the minor characters. If your hero is waiting on someone else's whim, now is the time to get him acting rather than reacting.

### REREAD DAY 3

Now read your pages 30 through 45.

Do you have all that is needed to get from the page 30 event to the initial growth on page 45?

Do you have a scene where she runs out and slams the door? Do you have a scene where he's acting in an old way within a new situation? Is your hero reacting to the events that are happening to him? These are all good uses of the end of Act II. Your scene on page 45 symbolically showing growth will tell you a lot. you will begin to see your script take on a life of its own.

In fact, page 45 is probably slightly different than what you planned. Do you think you don't even have that scene of initial growth on page 45? Find the line of dialogue where your character is telling you to catch up. The moment you find it, you take control of your script again.

This is the point where your character and you become two different people who can help each other. You, as author, must now be aware of your character's every move and every word, of dialogue so that you can *decide* if the action serves his best interests or not.

Here's an example: I have a client who's writing a mystery-thriller. The problem with the script is that the detective is too smart. He solves the mystery way before the end of the movie. This happens because the writer identifies with his character and wants him to be all-knowing. *You* as the writer can be all-knowing, that frees your character to learn as he goes. If he's smart enough in the beginning to know the end, then there's no story. So take control of the main character and allow him to learn; pace his discoveries along with the rest of the story.

Page 45 can be *your* initial growth moment, too. It's the time you will stop reacting to the script and start making active decisions on its behalf.

### I DON'T WANT TO

You might experience resistance today. You want to go out and play.

That's not unusual. These feelings are all functions of what you've accomplished on pages 30 to 45. This is the very point in the script when your character is experiencing all these reactions too.

If you and your character weren't growing you wouldn't be so scared. Being scared tells you there's not only initial growth already accomplished but major change occurring.

Okay. Read your pages 30 to 45 again and see if they convey the feelings you wanted. Read and re-read them until you *really* see what's there. Have you shown your character's denial, refusal, and resistance? And does he finally see old patterns in a new light and change his behavior? Clarify it. Take out everything that isn't your movie. Let your hero go forward, kicking and screaming if he must, but always forward.

Great! You're really on your way.

# DAY 13: REWRITE ACT II; PAGES 45–60

### TO RECAP

By page 45, your hero has reacted to what happened on page 30. He is now different, and we begin to see that here, in a symbolic scene. Also, by page 45 we begin to see a resolution of the original desire your character had on page 10. We're beginning to see how he's going to work this out.

Do you remember the children's story "The Little Engine That Could"? The engine chugs up the steep hill, repeating, "I think I can, I think I can"? Pages 45 to 60 should provide the same build-up. Your character is on his way to the top of the hill. Get him there.

### IF THE STORY IS SLIPPING THROUGH YOUR FINGERS, DO THIS

- Identify what your hero knows now that he didn't know in the random draft.
- Identify what *you* know now, as a result of the random draft, that might change your scenes?
- Eliminate scenes that repeat.
- Change dialogue that tells to actions that show.

If you see lines that tell you "I don't know what to do," change them to say "Here's the plan." Where you see lines of discussion ("Should we surround the house?") replace them with action (characters surround the house). Your hero could be scared, that's okay. He's still taking action. He is responding to all outside occurrences, not avoiding them.

From page 45, your hero is approaching a point of no return, page 60. So between pages 45 and 60, he might try to go back to see if his old life is there. He finds that it isn't. From 45 to 60 he is living "empty." That is, he's left how it was, but it isn't yet how it will be. So he's in between. It's uncomfortable to live "empty," so you will be tempted to take him back to what he knew, so he can know again why he left.

Watch to see if you have such scenes. Ask yourself if they legitimately belong in Act II. If you have bogged down today, it's probably because the "going home" scenes actually belong in Act I, before he leaves home. See if you can spot where the action stops because you're going back. If you want a "going back home" scene, rewrite to show how your character is different from how he was in Act One. *Inner Movie Axiom: Only go back to know to go forward.*

On page 60 is where he jumps off into midair. By now, he should have grown out of his old life so he can grow into his new one.

### JEOPARDY

In the recent past of movie making, it seemed that the only jeopardy big enough to scare us was the Mafia or the Russians or more recently, political terrorists.

But look to yourself. Are these real threats in your daily life?

True jeopardy, the interesting kind, is what we wrestle with in ourselves. Life and death. Love and abandonment. Success and failure. All manner of risk and loss. Being somebody, being nobody. When everything a person is and hopes to become is at stake, that makes for a strong sense of jeopardy.

You can find an external enemy for your hero to track and battle, but the real triumph will be his inner achievement.

Even with such a successful character as James Bond, who chases and foils the most powerful archenemies, we are watching the drama of a man who, given seemingly insurmountable obstacles, will not roll over and say, "Forget it. I'd rather give up and die than have to get out of this one." He is a hero because he's just not going to stop. So yes, go ahead, create an external enemy, but the real story rests with inner growth.

Look now to see where you put outer jeopardy. Take away the outer jeopardy and put it inside the hero to see what he's really up against (something in himself). Every time your story is lost, go find your character and put him back into the main action on screen.

### THE BLACK HOLE AND HOW TO FILL IT

Symptom: You are somewhere in the morass of Act II and you've lost it. There are twelve scenes in search of a story. Your hero is gone. You don't know where he went. You have scenes that follow minor characters off to Zanzibar.

Give the story back to the main character.

The villain is not the main character, don't let the villain *steal* the story.

Here's a one-minute assignment:

Take a scene from about page 55 that's missing your main character. Now, throw him into the scene. Have him say,

```
                    YOUR HERO
          This is my story and I'm taking it
          back.
```

Now what happens? Write that scene for one minute. Let him throw out the minor characters and idle action and have him take back the action and move it along.  ᴡᴡᴡᴡᴡᴡᴡᴡᴡᴡᴡᴡᴡᴡᴡᴡᴡᴡᴡᴡᴡ

**NOW YOU'RE TALKING.**

Somewhere in your one-minute movie is a line of dialogue expressing the commitment of your hero. She's "mad as hell and not going to take this anymore." She says, "I'm going to do this, don't even think of getting in my way."

Great. These are page-60 commitment lines. Look at the one you just discovered and look at the one you have on page 60. They both say the same thing, but at different levels of intensity.

Give that page-60 commitment line the highest intensity you can.

Okay, punch a pillow. Shadowbox in place. Go the distance. Rewrite pages 45 to 60.  ᴡᴡᴡᴡᴡᴡᴡᴡᴡᴡᴡᴡᴡᴡᴡᴡᴡᴡᴡᴡᴡᴡ

Here's the word for the day . . . .

Jump!

Tear through your pages with a machete.

Anything that looks like stoppage—surmount it. Any doubt —cut it out.

You need to go, go, go here, through major actions with major results.

And yet, this is getting tough. Are you tired? Do you want to see this done? That's how your hero feels. He's had it with all this uphill battle. *When does the dream come true?*

It's when he goes through these phases:

1 Commitment (page 60).

2 The stakes go up (pages 60–70), and he breaks through every obstacle using the new skills he's learned from the first half of Act II (pages 30–60).

3 He lets go (approximately page 72). He can give up because the obstacles are too much and too many, or he can let go when he chooses—before it does him damage. But he must let go. And that's because in the letting go he changes.

4 "It" happens.

Let's use *Rocky* as an example (even though this is not what occurs on *Rocky*'s page 75). Rocky realizes his challenge is bigger than he is. He realizes he's not going to win the fight. He takes two major actions. First he gives up that goal, and then he *changes his goal!* He *was* going to try to win the fight; *now* he's going to go the distance.

His goal was the championship, but winning now means going the distance, and he does. He stopped to have the realization that his goal wasn't going to happen and in that moment he changed his goal and learned that to win means to go the distance.

Find where you let your character give up. Then find the moment where he learns what he needs to solve the central question.

If you can't find it, let it go for the time being.

It will come to you.

## AND THEN HE REALIZES

In every story by a first-time screenwriter, he or she always uses the word "realizes." "And then he realizes" comes about page 75 in the story. It's your job to give us the specifics of *how* he realizes and *what* he realizes.

Rocky realizes he's not going to win because he sees the enormity of what he's up against with Apollo and then he sees *himself* in comparison. When he accepts the fact that he's a loser, he wins.

When we finally learn what we put ourselves through this for . . . our goal comes to us.

Go now—see something differently today. Write for eight minutes:

What I have learned about the story from writing this script is . . . . ▸▸▸▸▸▸▸▸▸▸▸▸▸▸▸▸▸▸▸▸▸▸▸▸▸▸▸▸▸▸▸▸▸▸

Now underline anything that jumps out at you.

What you underline is also the essence of what your character realizes.

Clarify that scene now.

This is a day to break through.

Jump! ▸▸▸▸▸▸▸▸▸▸▸▸▸▸▸▸▸▸▸▸▸▸▸▸▸▸▸▸▸▸▸▸▸▸▸▸

# DAY 15: REWRITE ACT II; PAGES 75–90

Today we need to get from the breakthrough on page 75 to the finish of Act II on page 90.

Does your hero seize the page 75 event as an opportunity and turn circumstances around to create an outcome in his favor?

Maybe you're writing a war movie. Your hero is being attacked and there's no way out. So he jumps on the tank and turns it on his enemies and wins the battle.

Does your character now turn reality around to suit his goal?

Look to see if he does. Have him go about facing his obstacles *in a whole new way*. He is changed, and the new way does work.

But let's make sure we can see it clearly.

Think of a time in your life when you mastered a difficult skill. It seemed hard at first and then became simple. There was a sudden click when it fell into place and became easy, effortless.

A would-be marathon athlete will train hard, feeling the pain as he concentrates on building a runner's body. And then one day when he is huffing and puffing around the track, he suddenly runs with the wind. That's mastery. That's what we're after here —the fluid rhythm of the karate expert, the lofty toss of the pizza dough thrower, the methodical rhythm of the supermarket cashier who moves his line out faster than the rest.

On pages 75 to 90, get us effortlessly through the crisis.

Look at the rhythm of the scenes. Have them build. Have them tie off earlier scenes. In Act I if your character was bullied; now let's see him get the best of the bullies. Show an early scene where they push him in the pond and then payoff that scene now by having him handle the same situation with a new attitude.

Let your hero show mastery now. If there is anything in pages 75 to 90 that looks like doubt or discussion or lack of movement, it doesn't belong here. It belongs before page 60.

The only decision he makes in this last section of Act II is the final one. The one that puts him over the top. The big one.

Now he can have the golden fleece. All he has to do is reach out and take it.

Play the major decision here. "Do I want what I came this far to get?" It is his if he wants it. No other decision belongs on these pages.

You've gotten through the challenge of Day 14. Now breeze, with confidence, through the triumph of Day 15.

You're smart now. You know what you're doing. Let's see you use your confidence on these pages.

See that your scenes are showing that confidence.

Change such dialogue as "I think I can" to a firm commitment. "This is the way I'm going to have it."

From pages 75 to 90 the crisis has heightened. Make the threat specific and the way your hero solves it precise. Have Act II culminate with the decision at hand and have your hero make it.

Show how he has grown.

Show the new guy we're dealing with. Show how everything *has* to work as he wants because now he just insists upon it.

Go. Be an expert. Let all the action fall into place beautifully. Take us to the start of the finish. ∾∾∾∾∾∾∾∾∾∾∾∾∾∾∾∾∾∾∾∾∾∾∾∾∾∾∾∾

# DAY 16: REWRITE ACT III; PAGES 90–100

The first time through Act III we went very fast. One day, thirty pages. You've got holes in this thing.

Excellent. That's exactly what you need.

Notice that the act of progressing through the rewrite draft has answered some important questions for your character.

Now ask yourself this: What's he going to get that he didn't plan on getting that is far better than what he hoped to get?

He knows something now he didn't know before. He's got the golden fleece. Now, having gotten it, what does it get him? What surprise is awaiting your main character and your audience?

In *Casablanca*, Bogart has the letters of transit, he has Ingrid Bergman, he has his bag packed, and he has burned all his bridges. He's leaving Casablanca. *But* he doesn't leave with Elsa; he leaves with Louie, to go off and help the war effort.

## THE CREATIVE ALTERNATIVE

Because of his renewed understanding of love ("We'll always have Paris. We didn't until you came to Casablanca."), Bogart is no longer a man with a thwarted heart. He is alive again, and he goes off to have a life. Something we thought could only happen *with* Elsa. But it happens *because* of her. The ending surprises us, and we're even satisfied by it!

So look now. Do you know your ending? Is it the same one you always had in mind? Is it predictable, inevitable? Are you satisfied?

If you think that your hero has two choices (he can either go or stay, get the girl or not get the girl), now is the time to let the *creative alternative* dawn on you. He will not get either one or the other, he will get something else entirely.

In *Splash*, Tom Hanks gets the girl but life is not how he thought it would be. He has to leave human life and live as a "merman." It's perfect. It solves all the problems he had adapting to her human behavior. Now all he has to do is adapt to being not human himself.

## WHAT IT TAKES TO CHANGE YOURSELF

We have spoken all the way through the rewrite about the change your character will go through. He is different in the end from what he was in the beginning. You have seen him go through all manner of obstacles to change. He has successfully surmounted the worst jeopardy you could think of.

We have sincerely worked to have him change. *Inner Movie Axiom: People don't change*.

Look at people around you. Look at yourself. You have been through tremendous changes writing this script. Look at all that has changed for you, and yet you are just more yourself.

*Inner Movie Axiom: People don't change—they grow.*

## THE DIFFERENCE BETWEEN CHANGE AND GROWTH

Growth is what happens inside you. You discover a new way to understand circumstances, and in seeing them a new way, the circumstances are changed.

I bring this up because of the "Hollywood ending."

## THE HOLLYWOOD ENDING

If the character becomes someone else in the end, who wants that? John Wayne fights the war and wins. The war's over. The end.

Can you picture him opening a hardware store in Kansas? No, this character is a war guy. He's going to go find another war. Let's say there's no war anywhere. *Things* change. He's got to open a hardware store. Twelve years later, somebody's going to come in and make trouble in the hardware store, and the Duke is going to be fighting and winning.

Circumstances change, behavior can change; he's still our everloving, rough-and-tumble Duke.

If you accept yourself, then you've got a chance at changing behavior, circumstances, attitude, self-esteem, everything.

*Inner Movie Axiom: We fear change because we think it's going to change us.*

Change doesn't destroy the person you are. Let your hero grow. Don't suddenly have a gambler stop gambling and become a family man in the last scene when he tried and couldn't change during all of Act II. Have him do it now, because he's grown and he's really ready to change. Let us believe it's going to work. Let your hero have an ending that is true to who he is *and* who he has become.

Go now, give your hero his best possible ending. ◆◆◆◆◆◆◆◆◆◆◆◆

Yesterday we talked about where you want your hero to go. Today let's get him there.

You want to get from the height of the crisis on page 90 to the end of your script as fast as you can. (P.S. Not all scripts are 120 pages. It's okay to tie up your Act III action fast and be done.)

There are certain closing duties you'll have to address. We need to give a conclusion to all the characters. In *Tootsie*, Michael had to go and apologize to Julie's father, who had proposed to him when he thought he was a her.

Whatever you started you now have to finish.

Conversely, now is also the time to make sure the seeds for the conclusion you're building towards were firmly planted in Act II.

For instance, when Katherine Ross goes with Butch and Sundance to Bolivia, she says she'll be with them but she won't watch them die. Later, they're at the campfire, nobody's looking at each other, and she says she thinks she'll leave on the next day's train.

Now we know that this is the doom scene. We know she's leaving because pretty soon they're going to die and she's not going to watch. Screenwriter William Goldman is a genuis at this kind of setup.

When you have your ending crystallized, start threading back through Act II and set us up for the payoff.

Don't create *new* Act II scenes. Just look at what you've got and rearrange a line of dialogue to foreshadow the end.

In *Splash* there is a great scene between the brothers played by John Candy and Tom Hanks. John tells Tom to go ahead and love Madison. In the end, when Tom finds out he can never come back to land, not even for Christmas to be with his brother, we know it's okay with John, because he had already said to go ahead and choose love. So the relationship between the brothers is resolved way back in an early scene. We don't have to have Tom stop everything in the end to run and say goodbye.

If you are having trouble with Act III structure, there is a formula you can use to get you through. Break the act down into beginning, middle, end. Have page 93 be the central question, restated; have the character's desire realized by page 100; show his commitment to a new life by page 110 and a new surprise addition to that life by page 115. Use this formula as a guide only, there's no need to obsess over it.

The easy way to end is to have the final three pages provide a kind of companion bookend to the beginning three pages. If your hero moved in on page 1, he's moving out on page 120.

Answer the central question.

▶▶▶▶▶▶▶▶▶▶▶▶▶▶▶▶▶▶▶▶▶▶▶▶▶▶▶▶▶▶▶▶▶▶◀

And then

FADE OUT.

# DAY 18: TWEAK ACT I

Rah rah sis boom bah! You've done it! You've gotten through. It lives. You are a truly spectacular human being.

So now what?

Now we tweak.

### THE DIFFERENCE BETWEEN A BIG TWEAK AND A LITTLE TWEAK

If you are confident that you've gotten the story and the pages are pretty clean, meaning:

- no holes,
- no questions,
- cause and effect builds,
- what is set up is paid off, and
- you're satisfied,

then you'll be doing a little tweak today.

If this is your first screenplay and you're still not sure if the story's there, then you'll do a big tweak.

### HOW TO DO A LITTLE TWEAK

Have ready the script in a neat pile. If this requires that you take it to a typist and get a clean copy back, then stop the 21-day clock and get that done. (Don't allow the clock to stop for more than three days.)

If you are the typist, type *before* tweaking. Don't stop the 21-day clock and don't allow more than one day to type. The rule is that while the script is in your hands it takes 21 days to finish, if it's in somebody else's hands, it's their business how long it takes.

If you are your own typist, do not tweak and type simultaneously. You will never finish either.

Now. Let's assume you're ready with a clean copy of your script and a pen with ink of a color you especially like. Choose a place to do the read through. This should be somewhere that is *not* your usual work space. Turn on background music if you haven't until now; make this time and place somewhat different from your regular writing environment.

Now do a marathon read through. Have the pen on the table, not in your hand. If something needs fixing, pick up the pen, fix it, then put the pen down until the next thing needs fixing. This is so you won't change every "it" to "the" and cross out and put back. Remember, this is a marathon read through. Do it in one sitting. Get the big picture.

1. Look out for logistical flaws. If she calls New York from L.A., do you have a three-hour time difference? If you left him in the rain, do you have him walk into the next scene wet?

2. Read for pace. Does it bog down anywhere? If so, see where the dialogue repeats and cut, cut, cut. If characters are arguing, have them stop and get on with the action, or at least have action going on under the argument.

3. If dialogue seems too on-the-nose, use subtext. For instance, if he's saying he's going to leave her, what happens to the scene if you have her seducing him, or if she's throwing his clothes in his suitcase and shoving him out the door? Subtext is what gives meaning to the dialogue.

4. See if one long deadly scene can be broken up and spread out over different times and locations. This is film; let's be cinematic. Cut to here and there and tomorrow. Free up the linear line.

5. Now that you know what it's about, ask yourself if this is the best possible way to do the scene. Could it be in a helicopter, instead of in the kitchen? Could it be shown with no dialogue? Could the dialogue be entirely different?

6. Look at scenes that don't seem to work. Is there a split-second story here that could be conveyed better? Is there a choice you can make that will instantly show a thousand feelings going on?

### HERE'S HOW TO DO A BIG TWEAK

Do it the same way you would a little tweak, only do it at your desk on the original pages. Don't retype until after you've tweaked. You are allowed to hold the pen in your hand and use it a lot or use your computer or typewriter. What you will be doing is a line by line edit of all action and dialogue to make the best possible choices to tell your story.

Here are some guidelines for tweaking Act I:

1. Tighten and retighten the first ten pages. Take out any little thing that isn't absolutely necessary.

2. Punch up the dialogue to say as clearly as possible what you really want it to say.

3. Check the central life questions *again*. Have you said what you want to say loud and clear?

4. Look at descriptions; if three words can be replaced with one, do it.

5. If it's a comedy, now is the time to make it funnier. Cut on punchline. For example, in *Private Benjamin*, Goldie Hawn says to her dashing dancing partner, "I can't go with you, I don't even know you." He says, "I'm a gynecologist, I'm Jewish . . . " CUT TO: The two in bed together. Film gives you an opportunity to use time change to make a joke. Use it. Be hilarious.

6. How well are you laying in exposition? Are you having the character say, "This is my birthday and it's the Depression and I'm an orphan"? Show, don't tell. Have her sing "Happy Birthday" to herself when she finds a candle in the garbage. Find your exposition and take it out of dialogue and put it in action. If you must tell us, find a minor character to be the narrator. For instance, the hero goes for a job, the minor character as the personnel director tells us the hero's qualifications and what the job is that he'll be doing.

7. Is your hero in most of the scenes from pages 10 through 30? If not, why not?

Here's the main action for today:

Tweak away everything that isn't your movie.

### WHEN YOU DON'T KNOW
### WHAT YOU'RE TRYING TO TALK ABOUT

You're somewhere deep in the morass of Act II and you've lost it. You are attached to that scene and this character and you've read it over and over and you can't find where to fix it. Here's a magical solution:

Read two pages of a section that's not right, a section you've read a thousand times before. Notice that what the characters are saying to each other is said three times.

Their words are marching in place:

> HE
>
> So, should we go?

> SHE
>
> I don't know.

> HE
>
> Do you want to?

> SHE
>
> What will I wear?

> HE
>
> If we're going, we should go.

> SHE
>
> I don't know what to wear.

Identify the marching in place and draw a square around it and X it out:

> HE
>
> So, should we go?

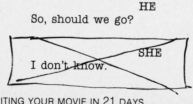

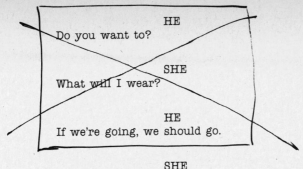

HE
Do you want to?

SHE
What will I wear?

HE
If we're going, we should go.

SHE
I don't know what to wear.

Now go through your entire section that is dead and awful and "Xorcize" the dead stuff.

### WHAT TO DO WHEN YOU'VE LOST IT

Are you feeling overwhelmed? Are you anxious, jumping out of your skin? Before you is a mountain of strange papers. You find yourself shouting, "I've written garbage pages! They don't mean anything!"

Good—you are progressing. This is an indication that it's time to change modes.

Remember: You do not have to begin at the beginning again. You have done that.

Go to your visual aid again. Sit down, calm down, reconnect with your initial passion for this story. Get that feeling again. Do not think. Do not ask questions. Empty your mind of all trying-to-figure-it-out. Empty your mind of all the judgments it's making.

Your job here is to rekindle the original *feeling*. Close your eyes and *feel* the story again.

After you've gone back, after you remember why you were doing this in the first place, go forward. See that you aren't stuck. See that you are at a junction and can move on. Do you have a thousand scenes and no story? Are all your papers on backs of envelopes? Do they look like they've been chewed? Stop. Clean it up. Type it up. Sleek it down.

In order to identify areas that need tweaking, let's go back to your life. It's the shortest distance between finding out what needs fixing and fixing it.

## WHERE ARE YOU IN ACT II OF YOUR LIFE?

Are you reacting to external circumstances (pages 30 to 45)?

Are you experiencing initial growth (pages 45 to 60)?

Are you committing yourself to your goal (page 60)?

Are you about to change (page 75)?

Are you resolving your old life and taking on a new one (page 90)?

Where you are in your life shows you where you need to tweak in the script.

*Did you have some conflict determining if this movie should be commercial or personal?* Are you having difficulty with loved ones. Are they asking, "When are you going to get a real job?" You're determined, but this seems to be an uphill battle. You're not getting much outside support.

Your Act II is probably a humdinger. Your hero is going through the deepest bowels of hell and not surfacing. Act II is overlong. It is one test after the other, and you are putting you and your hero through the same hell over and over.

Lighten up. Have him pass his tests from pages 45 to 60. You can let him triumph now. Notice where you can consolidate scenes after page 60. In fact, it's a bit lopsided here. You have him commit earlier than page 60, and then there seems to be another commitment scene closer to page 75 and lots of tests in between. After you consolidate the tests you put him through, "realize" that the first commitment scene was really a false gesture on his part. He's beating his chest and making promises but he knows he can't handle it yet. He's just strutting stuff he knows he doesn't have. Eliminate that. Don't have him commit until he means it. And by the way, he can be scared, it's okay. He just has to be sincere.

*Is your character protesting that he's going to buck all odds and nobody's going to stop him?* That's fine, except now you find that nobody is trying to. State clearly what he's fighting for and see where you can show clearly that there's something keeping him from it.

*Does your Act II want to keep going back to Act I?* You're never sure if it isn't all backstory. Focus on pages 30 to 45. Get to that initial growth scene and you'll be alright. Let all the later scenes build from that.

When you see your character becoming ambivalent, make a decision for him. Where you and your hero were one in the random draft now you control your characters; don't let them get out of control.

Find that initial growth scene around page 45 and don't let him go backward after that. Say your main character is already in childbirth. You can have her say, "This is too hard. I'm going home." But she can't, she's got to stay there and have the baby. Keep going forward.

*You might be experiencing a lot of heebie-jeebies about what your character learns on page 75.* You feel resistance to change. Here's a fine cure. Repeat this statement: "I approve of myself." Repeat that about a thousand times in the next few minutes. Now reread Day 6 and Day 15. Then fix Act II. I swear it will work.

### GO AHEAD AND SAY IT

You will find that there is something that you wanted to state *very* strongly. Something you *really* care about. And you stated it here, somewhere in Act II. Only now you see that it's not really there yet. You want to take it out completely. Here's what to do instead. Make it stronger!

If your character is in the back of the room whispering, bring him out in front and have him say it loud and clear. You don't want him to be absent or weak or pretending. Wake him up and keep him awake. Write the juicy scene that expresses your passion for doing this.

Now put in the scene that you avoided. For instance, if his estranged wife comes to see him, does he run out the door? Have the confrontation. Once you write the scene and get it out, you can see what really needs saying here. Then find a good way to show that.

### PRE-CLOSING CEREMONIES

A word about your deadline: It is your friend.

Focus to reach your deadline. Make it your priority. Sleep, food, and phone are secondary to the deadline. Pace yourself. If you get to the finish line and you're not finished, do this: take a moment to feel like a jerk because you missed the deadline. Then reorganize based on what you have left to do.

If you don't do that, it will take more time to finish; your body is geared for a Monday completion, and if you keep going through Wednesday your body will get confused and walk off the job. Don't think we're suggesting that you actually miss your deadline; we are just in the process now of beginning to end.

### LET'S TALK ABOUT OUTCOME

There's something to do today. There is life beyond your movie.

Write for 8 minutes:

What am I going to do when my movie is done? (I mean beyond selling it and making a million dollars. I know you're going to do that. I mean what are you going to do on Day 22?)

Are you going to celebrate? Do the laundry? Quit your job? Get married? What? You need to know you have a life to go to when this is over with.

So write on that for 8 minutes.

Okay. On the heels of your 8 minutes on Life After Script, answer this multiple-choice question.

What is your overriding feeling while tweaking?

1  The script's a mess, you have no idea what you have.

2  It may be brilliant. It may be awful. You're not sure which.

3  You think you should go back to the beginning and start a new story.

4  All of the above.

What you are experiencing is closing anxiety. Any problems in finishing are not problems in the script.

### IS THIS TRUE FOR YOU?

Do you tend to start projects and not always finish? Then be on the lookout for this:

You might have gotten to Act II and suddenly another story started. And Act III almost looks like Act I all over again. See if this is so.

### IT'S A COMMON FEELING

The concept of death probably frightens you profoundly. You feel that if you finish anything, it means you will die. (I've worked with *many* writers who feel this way. You're not alone.) But here's what. It's not death that you are afraid of—it's more life. If you can take your character from point *a* to point *z* and are *willing* for him to experience unknown adventures along the way, then he will not end in death; he will end up more alive. Not surprisingly, we often think that if we set out from point *a* to get to point *z*, that's all we'll get and that's the end. Point *z* is *never* all we get. So put your hero on the roadway. Give him life.

Here's what to do if you're afraid:

Just do it.

*Inner Movie Axiom: The success of the Act III tweak is directly proportional to your desire to get the thing done.*

# DAY 21: CLOSING CEREMONIES

Let's talk for a minute about this business of the 21 Days.

The Inner Movie method is designed so you can write a movie in 21 days. But here's what: There's no law that says you have to. You can take anywhere from three weeks to a lifetime to do it. Whatever *you* want. But if you want to do it in 21 days, you can.

If you want to take longer, you can. But still use the 21-Day procedure. The concept still works. Go fast through the random draft; then take off an arbitrary amount of time, then rewrite, then rest again, and then polish.

Don't think too much about your movie.

*Inner Movie Axiom: The longer you take; the longer you'll take.* It's actually easier to do it faster.

I bring this up because if you got here and you're not done, you didn't flunk. Keep going. It will get done.

### HOW TO KNOW WHEN YOU'RE DONE

Here are 9 test questions that can be answered only when the script is absolutely finished.

Ask yourself:

1 What is my story? Can I state it in two or three brief sentences giving the beginning, the middle, and the end?

2 Who is my main character and what does he want?

3 What does my main character get? How is that different from what he wanted?

4 Can the reader state my story and identify the main character's needs by page 10?

5 Is it in screenplay form—120 pages, correct tabs, specific descriptions, appropriate caps, paginated?

6 What haven't I said that I really want to say?

7 Is it the story I wanted to tell?

8 Do I believe it?

9 What have I learned? How is it different from what I visualized it would be?

## HOW TO PICK TWO PEOPLE FOR A TEST READING
## (EXCLUDING ALL MEMBERS OF YOUR IMMEDIATE HOUSEHOLD)

Pick out experts in the field. If you don't have access to an expert, your best bet is a kid between the age of ten and twelve. "Pitch" your story to the kid verbally. He or she will be able to tell you if you are missing any story points. The reason ten- to 12-year-olds are good at this is because they are at the height of their brain coordination and language skills. It's the time the parts of the brain are still cooperating with one another naturally. Verbal channels are open. After twelve years old, we all start shutting down around ego and opinion. (If the studios really want to hire baby moguls, this is the age range they should interview.) Kids are really good at story.

If no expert or kid is available, then choose a wise friend who is insightful about you. What he or she doesn't know about structure can be made up for in an understanding of the uniqueness that you bring to the story.

While they are reading, make up a list of at least twenty questions you want to ask. What you want to know is this: Did they receive the movie that you thought you sent?

Stop them after page 10 and ask if they know the story. What is it about? Have them tell you everything they know so far.

Where you have any doubts about the script, think of questions that will reveal whether they got what you wanted them to get:

- Do you care what happens to the characters?
- Are their problems interesting to you?
- Whose story is it?
- Do you know what happens next?
- Do you care what happens next?
- Does it lose your interest?
- Where does it lose your interest?
- Can you describe him/her?
- Can you tell his backstory?
- Does he grow?
- What happens in Act II?
- Are you still interested?

- What do you think will happen?
- What do you want to happen?
- Does he talk too much?
- Does he not talk enough?
- What if he were ten years older?
- Did the villain scare you?
- Was there enough of a threat?

So now, list twenty questions you want to ask the reader to find out if you said what you wanted to say; then list twenty questions you want the reader ask you, questions that will help you find out if you've said it the best possible way.

You are not after unbridled praise here. You want your script to be the best you can make it.

When you finish with one test reading, digest what you've learned and do a second. See where the issues come up again. Decide what needs fixing and fix it. Do not fix anything you don't want to fix. When you are finished with two test reads, solidify the script and stand behind what you've got. Declare it done.

### PUTTING IT OUT TO PEOPLE

"I can't send this out to the public. If I reveal myself, people won't like me."

We think if somebody knows us they're automatically not going to like us. The opposite is true. We can't possibly like you unless we know you.

Do you feel you can't take criticism? Well, of course you can't. Why should you? You're doing what you need to be doing when you need to be doing it. No matter what you're doing or what the script is, it's exactly what it needs to be.

### HOW TO NOT TAKE CRITICISM

Don't ask "Is it good or "Can I write?" You'll get a subjective answer. You'll get *opinions*.

*Inner Movie Axiom: Opinions have more to do with the one who has the opinion than with the thing he or she has the opinion about*.

If you are talking with an agent, the question is not "Is it good?" The question is "Can you sell it?"

They will give you their opinions anyway. It will be about the impending merit of your property. It's not personal.

Here are two ways to be judged:

Know what you wanted your audience to get from your story, then ask your reader if he got that. If he did, you've succeeded. If he didn't, fix it. You see how you need to keep the power of judgment with yourself. Next, if you're brave enough, and you promise not to go on needing approval, ask some questions about what the reader would have liked more of or less of. What would have helped him to understand the story better? Notice you are not saying, "You hated my story, didn't you, didn't you?" You are asking, "What story did *you* want to see?"

You need to stay alert concerning the response to your work. This is a vulnerable time for a writer. You don't know yet if you can write. A part of finding out is to measure the response of others to your writing.

*But*, self-doubt can only be answered by you. No matter how many people you show your script to, no matter how glowing their praise, it won't do you any good until you decide *for yourself* what you have achieved.

*Inner Movie Axiom: Self-esteem is something you have to give to yourself.* That's why it's called *self*-esteem. What you get from others is something else entirely.

Here's a freeing thought about your work:

It doesn't have to be all things to all people. It just has to satisfy you.

### FINAL CHECK POINT

If you still aren't sure if it's done try this test. You will have one of two attitudes about your script. 1. You need to call in a swat team to pry it out of your hands. Or 2. You don't want to look at it again until a studio pays you to rewrite.

Which attitude shows you that you're done?

Did you say number two? Actually it's number one. Your script is done when you still love it and can still find yet another layer to peel back and explore. It's done now because you've got it to where it is alive. And it *will* continue to grow, but now it can grow out of your typewriter and into the marketplace.

The other one, number two, is the one that still needs work.

When you think you've gone as far as you can go, you haven't gone far enough. You've stopped just short of bringing the thing to life. The fact that you don't want to look at it again shows that you're tired, it doesn't show that you're done.

It's okay. Go ahead, give yourself recess; then ask yourself the hardest question of all . . . "Am I willing to go the extra mile?" If you are willing, then hello, you are a writer.

### AND WHEN YOU'RE REALLY, REALLY DONE

Aren't you good!

You got ready.

You struggled.

You pushed.

You believed in yourself/had no hope.

You exercised/lounged around;

Ate right/devoured the refrigerator;

Dreamed about it/had nightmares;

Thought about it/didn't think about it;

Tried/stopped trying;

Avoided/kept at it;

Had flashes it would be brilliant/watched it disappear;

Been brave around it/been a coward;

Wrote/couldn't write;

And finally it was done . . . a cinch.

Nothing to it!

Hats and horns! Hooray! Voila! Aren't you the best possible person in the world?

You had a party after the random draft, you can have another one now. But here's how this celebration is different:

For the first-draft party, you needed people to congratulate you; to agree you were a writer, to help, support, and encourage. This celebration is a thank-you to them and to yourself for having done all that.

Now you *are* a writer. You did it. How you celebrate is up to your imagination, but here's one thing that will be the true ending, and the beginning of all things new:

You will experience a very private moment when, without coaxing, you will be very *very* pleased with yourself. It will be a golden moment and it belongs to you alone. Life will go on exactly as it has been going on, but from that moment forward you will be forever different.

The Inner Movie Method toasts your golden moment.

# Embracing the Impossible Obstacles

# ZEN AND
# THE HIGH ART OF
# GETTING THE THING DONE

**Oh you poor dear**

You've come to this section to look up why you've stopped. Is it because . . .

"I can't write, my day job drains me."

"I can't write, my teenage son just dyed the dog purple."

"I can't write, my psoriasis is flaring up."

"I can't write, everyone is against me and *I'm* not even on my side."

There, there. Give yourself a sweet hug. It's okay to feel all manner of anxiety. There's a lot on you here. You're only changing your life. This is *important* to you.

*Inner Movie Axiom: Always treat yourself the best possible way that you can.*

Be a comfort to yourself. This is actually an assignment.

Feel the feelings, no matter how lousy, because in feeling them we can then identify their roots and in identifying them we can then solve them.

Here's the situation:

It's taken everything you've got to get yourself to sit down to the blank page. You have declared once and for all that you are a writer! Nothing can stop you! And now you find yourself nodding off.

Writing a screenplay, writing anything, is hard work. It's hard enough just doing the work required, let alone coping with all the heebie-jeebies involved.

Remember, you are a writer. You are creative. What you might have created are ways to stop.

This is the section where we Embrace the Impossible Obstacles. You can look up where you've stopped, identify the block, and take new action to keep going.

These blocks are divided into outer obstacles and inner obstacles. The first section, on outer obstacles, covers time and place and page count. You'll find ways to handle the hard time you get from your spouse, your kids, and your boss. The section on inner obstacles covers the hard time you give yourself.

Writing is an art form because it uses two different parts of you: your head and your heart. Blockage arises when you are using primarily one when the other needs to predominate. If the parts of yourself are not in harmony, you get blocked, and there is practically nothing in the world that feels worse. So, since we absolutely want you to feel great, we'll identify your obstacle and embrace it, because . . .

*Inner Movie Axiom: Obstacles are only there in case you care to stop.*

# HOW TO PAY THE RENT
# WHILE PAYING YOUR DUES

### Keeping the day job

Maybe you have a job in the buzz saw department at Sears. Maybe you're not happy there and that's why you want to write a script, make a million dollars, and leave the job that doesn't foster your creativity. Maybe you're haunted by these questions:

- Should you quit to write the script?
- Should you tough it out and write on weekends?
- Should you wait?
- Should you forget the whole thing and stay put?

Of course you're not going to stay put, or you wouldn't be reading this book. And of course you're not going to wait, because . . .

### There's no such thing as waiting

Waiting implies an inactive, undisclosed, random amount of time spent hoping that sooner or later your life situation will be more favorable and you can pursue your dream. There's no such thing as waiting, because life will go on without you.

It's time. Decide on action. Take a step into your future.

## How to make your day job work for you

Organize your job so that you can put it on automatic pilot. Eventually you will leave it, but now you're going to change it.

If one of the dread factors of your job is tension with your co-workers, you are now going to detach. This means you will be getting along with that co-worker you can't stand. Here's how: You have a secret they don't know, you're writing your movie. You're taking action to get out of this job, and you're still in it only because now the job is working for you.

## All you've got to do is show up

Getting enjoyment from any job is a matter of attitude. The true perks on a job are the ones you give yourself.

Giving a job what is required is plenty enough to keep you busy. Just getting there in the morning everyday takes tremendous fortitude. You don't need to invent other requirements.

If you are there laying your heart on the line, you're going to be unhappy because you want an equal response in return. *But that wasn't the deal!* You were only promised a paycheck. Accepting this frees you up to experience such life affirming behavior as smiling. Enjoy and benefit from the experience.

*Inner Movie Axiom: If you keep all the little rules, you're free to break all the big ones.*

## How to live a double life

There is something uplifting about the secret you have. Something you're working for now gives you a new way to be at your job. *You* are not invested in it anymore. *It* is there to serve you.

A job does something else. It gives you structure so that you don't have time to get overwhelmed worrying about your script. Notice how you can use your job to help you write. When you drive to work, can that be organizational time? Find pockets of writing time in your work day. Run your movie on your inner projector. What scenes can you finish before lunch? Answer questions about character as you watch co-workers.

See the whole picture. Then chunk it out. Divide it into

8-minute parts. Make a list of these. Write a scene, a page, or a line of dialogue between phone calls and the demands of the day. Lead a double life.

Through the act of writing your script you will be outgrowing your day job. Chances are you won't be fired until you're ready to go. Gauge when. Usually if you think you can't stand it for another minute, it opens up and there's more there to draw from. The best time to leave a job is when you are ready to leave. Don't let them fire you until the moment you're ready to go.

Meanwhile use the Xerox machine for script copies. This is illegal. This is immoral. This is advisable. You need to feel you are gleaning some benefit from your job; otherwise you can't continue to be there. And we need you to be there for the moment. Keep it. Now proceed to *grow out of it*.

## Barter

I was working on a production in an office for two weeks while needing to finish a movie script. There was a secretary typing madly. I noticed she was typing the same article four times. She said she loved to type but there just wasn't anything to do but answer the occasional phone, so I gave her my movie pages to type and we were both ecstatic. I treated her to a sumptuous lunch and she handed me a perfectly typed script in return. *Bartering* is one of the all-time synergistic pleasures of life. Let someone who loves the work do the work, while you do the work you love.

## What happens when you get fired

Congratulations! This is exactly what you wanted. But knowing you, here's what you will think:

> YOU
> I'm such a jerk I can't even keep a
> junk job that I didn't even want.

You will be very hard on yourself. This is your way of showing yourself that you are responsible. You fear that if you don't come down hard on yourself your loved ones will.

I knew it. Deep down you're really a
vagrant.

Settle this. If the job is gone, don't let it continue to take your energy. You are free.

## When you quit your job

If you think you have no time because you have a high-pressure job, quit, and then you'll see that you will still have no time! You learn this when you have all the time in the world. There is always something.

See the section on time, money, and hypochondria. You will have questions about all three. You will have very few questions on your writing, which, if you'll remember, was why you quit in the first place.

Not to worry—settle in, *then* pick up the pencil.

## What to do when unemployment runs out

Good. You've been living as though the other shoe would drop, now there's action to take.

Here's your choice: You can get a day job again and balance your time between writing and the job. But you already did that once, and you're scared that the script will turn to dust. This won't happen, however, because *this* day job you'll get because you *have to*—and *you're mad*. And *mad* is the best thing you can be right now. Because what you are adjusting to is not that you don't have enough money but that you don't have enough time.

## More time than money/more money than time

You will feel the need to budget your money. This is well and good. However, this will keep you broke.

When you quit your job you think that having saved up money will buy you time. If money buys you time, how much are you paying yourself for each one of your hours? You can eat up a year of your time with the money you have saved, but what was your salary? Minimum wage or less? That is not sound economical use of a year. Appreciate the value of *time* and what each hour costs. The way to be rich is to notice this. People who are broke have all the time in the world. They can talk on the phone. They can bang at your door. People who are rich have very little spare time. Their time is utilized, filled, they get *value for their hour*. How much are you paying for each of your valuable hours?

## When your money runs out

Linda quit her job to write. Now her money's running out and she needs to work again. She asked me if I knew anyone who could give her a menial job in "the business" while she kept writing. Usually I would dive into my Rolodex and start giving out phone numbers, but something here didn't feel like progress. I found out this was her modus operandi, taking junk job after junk job so she could write—but she wasn't writing. Now here she was again. So I gave her an assignment: "Stop it." Look at the pattern of your behavior. *Inner Movie Axiom: If it doesn't work, don't do it again.*

## Find a better way

When our plan doesn't work, we think we failed. So we go at it again in the same way, only this time harder.

You can see this when a vending machine takes your quarter. You hit it. It doesn't give you your quarter back, so you hit it harder.

*When the plan doesn't work, change the plan.*

## The difference between a junk job, a job job, and a real job

Decide now.

Do you want a junk job that pays the rent but doesn't tax your mind, so that you can still write when you get home?

Do you want a job job where you have a business card but not so much responsibility that you don't feel free to write?

Do you want a real job, where you *are* the job and it takes your creative attention?

The difference is in how much of yourself you're willing to commit to the job.

My contention is, no matter what job you have you can't help but bring your whole self to it. Avoidance *takes* energy; involvement *gives* you energy.

If you do the job with joy you can also write after hours.

The Inner Movie Method was designed so you can write whether you have a junk job, a job job, a real job, or no job. What job you have has nothing to do with what keeps you from writing.

Arrange your circumstances to work in your favor.

One student went from junk jobs to a real job, so she could make more money. But then she had no time. She wanted to quit. She hated it. We made a schedule—she had two weeks to turn her circumstances around so that she could keep her job and she would stop hating it. She needed to arrange to have enough energy after work so that she could focus on her writing. In two weeks she moved the furniture, delegated tasks, standardized procedures, and manuevered a ten-hour, four-day work week, so that she had a block of three days off for herself. She now loves the job and is on Day 16 of her script.

## I have to write my script and sell it to pay next month's rent

This will not happen. Money worries will sap your spirit and creativity. The energy it takes to scramble for your next meal is energy you need to put into your script instead.

If you are living on somebody else's couch, down to the last of your clean underwear, and you think that the solution to your money problems is to write your script—*don't*. Take care of your circumstances first. Then start writing.

## How much money is enough?

Financial freedom is having money enough so you don't need money.

That doesn't always mean a million dollars; sometimes it means ninety-two cents for a taco.

# TIME

### How to give yourself more writing time—
### the either/or energy split

It takes 100 percent of your efforts just to clear enough space in reality for you to even *be* a writer in the first place. Then, after you've finally cleared the spot and the moment is yours, the first thing you do is fall asleep. It's okay, the climb to this stage made you tired. Strike a balance between resting up and keeping your position—decide not to fall back. Rest and go forward. It takes one-third of your overall writing energy just to keep the world far enough away so that you are able to concentrate while writing and still close enough so that you can go out and live when your day's work is done.

Here's a riddle: What is the one thing that we all have exactly as much of as everybody else in any given day? Rich or poor, high-powered, busy luminary or anybody—what do we all have that is exactly equal? We all have twenty-four hours in a day.

So if we have the exact same amount and some among us *found* time and *took* the time to write, then it can't be that there's no time, it must be that there are *choices*.

Now let's assume you agree that it is choice, and you choose to have six kids and a dog and you also choose writing. How do you work that out?

Don't fight it.

Look at your time and how you spend it. Chances are, a great deal of your time is spent thinking and feeling that you have no time. Stress is usually your mind worrying about how you're going to handle all the stuff you have to do tomorrow, today.

Are you overworked this minute? If you are, you can take an action this minute to work it out. If this minute's stress has to do with future minutes, you're choosing to spend time nonproductively. If it takes 80 percent of your entire energy to keep the door shut on the world long enough so you can write, that only leaves you with 20 percent to use on the writing.

If you're overwhelmed—surrender to it. Walk your kindergartner to school, but bring along your pad and paper. Always say yes to life.

## How I cured myself of seasickness

I have been known to hang over the rail of the great yachts of the world. On a recent sailing day, before I even left the harbor, I caught myself bracing against wooziness.

> ME
> Wait a minute, are you sick this minute?

> ME
> No!

> ME
> Then if this is a "well" minute, don't infuse it with sickness.

I decided to not worry about it until it happened, and it never happened.

Take care of one thing at a time—that's you—and one day at a time—that's now.

## How to hear yourself think

Listen and you will tell yourself everything you need to know. As you become aware of how character is revealed when you observe others, become aware of yourself too. What's on your heart's mind. Listen.

Notice the noise in your life. Distractions are infinite. It's a way of staying in the old place. For instance, have you said, "I want to be alone"? The first moment you're alone do you call a friend to say "I want to be alone"?

Give yourself air and light. We all need a lot of it.

## Letting your mind go on without you

                    YOU
I don't have time to think.

                    INNER MOVIE
Good. Thinking gets you into trouble.
Don't do it.

# PLACE AND STUFF

### Paraphernalia

Last Tuesday I couldn't continue. I had an uncontrollable urge to run right out and buy an electric pencil sharpener. When someone takes up a new sport in this country, their first sign of physical activity is a trip to the bike shop or club house to buy the *paraphernalia* of the sport. You haven't taken a swing at the ball yet, but you've spent $62.50 on the shoes and hat. Buying a tool or a piece of equipment is often the first commitment to the game. And it's a right instinct. Go ahead—commit retail. You sometimes need external, tangible proof that you are committing yourself to an activity. If you are a writer and you haven't written anything yet, you need to look like a writer. You need to have a writer's place to sit.

I lived on a Greek island. A friend lent me her Hermes portable typewriter. She called me "clickety-clack" because you could hear it all over the island. I had a tiny Greek table and chair and I sat on the veranda overlooking the Aegean. Just before Greek Orthodox Easter, everyone on the island whitewashes the houses. No one asked me to help with the whitewashing. I attribute this to the fact that I had a place and stuff that said I was a writer and I was working. I was grateful. Writing is hard but whitewashing is manual labor. Oh no!

## Where to arrange workspace

You can be as elaborate or spartan as your personality dictates. One student turned her guest room into an office. It took two months. Great. It was a gestation period. The act of preparing her workspace got her thinking about the script. When she was done decorating she started writing. Just make sure you stop getting ready and start writing.

Another student has a portable typewriter and writes at lunchtime in her car at the park. I have an office that looks like corporate headquarters with a computer and printer that each have their own furniture, but every afternoon I leave all that and take my pen and paper and go write on the beach.

But a fixed place *is* important. Put a visual aid there. Be able to leave it all out because the act of putting it away means you have to take it out and having to take it out—you just won't. We have statistics to prove it.

If you have no place, then find the place in a thing like a red notebook.

This place and stuff arranging doesn't have to be expensive. I have a huge crockery mug the color of money. I have a 3 A.M. sweater.

So go now. Shop.

# SHOULD I HAVE
# A WRITING PARTNER,
# AND HOW DO I CHOOSE ONE?

The best thing about a writing partner is that he'll say the "stupid idea" you were thinking but didn't dare say. Once you hear the stupid idea, you're inspired to think of the next brilliant fragment of it. One stupid idea plus one next fragment can equal a great collaboration.

A partnership is a very intimate marriage of talents, needs, desires, work habits, and personal hygiene. Ask yourself, are you emotionally compatible as a team? If one is down and one is up, does the down one have the ability to pull the up one down, or does the up one have the ability to pull the down one up? If you can't support one another emotionally, don't count on this support as part of the partnership. Set the time, and the place, and the amount of pages you'll do, then cultivate emotional support from an outside source.

### The prospective writing partner's
###    compatibility quiz

Ask yourself these questions. There is no perfect score. It's up to you to decide the perfect partnership.

- Are you both willing to succeed at the same rate?
- Is he/she ready for the same success that you're ready for?

- When you brainstorm is it exciting? Do ideas fly about that you both love?
- Chances are you'll be opposites. One takes the notes, sets the time. The other has the ideas, then escapes out of the door to the chiropractor. Do you bring out the best or the worst in each other?
- Is there one smoker and one non-smoker?
- Is one a day person and the other a night person?
- Is one good at structure, the other good at dialogue?
- Are you stronger together than separately?
- Do you like each other?
- Is there "always something" taking your writing time (e.g., his back goes out, then a cold, then a wedding to go to in Kansas)?
- Do you have a shared vision of what you want from working together?
- Do you agree on the future you plan for your shared career?
- Does either partner have a loved one who will be jealous of the time you spend together?
- Together do you create personal drama rather than finished pages?

## Which one is the writer?

Deep down, you will always wonder how much of the magic is you and how much is the other guy. Here's the truth: it's both of you coming together. You have to be willing to appreciate that something happens between the two of you that wouldn't happen separately. If you are not willing to share that unique magic that happens as a result of being together, then don't engage in a partnership.

## Proving yourself

Do you feel that you need to prove yourself? Forming a partnership to do that won't work. How can you use someone else to prove yourself? You have to do that alone. Partnerships formed under these circumstances generally end bitterly, each person thinking that he contributed the most to the screenplay and the other stole the idea.

## Vows

When you enter into a professional partnership involving the career decisions of two self-supporting adults, you will probably consider this a very serious commitment. Here is how my friend Ron Fricano and I entered into negotiations to become partners:

> RON
> Wanta write together?

> ME
> Okay.

We toasted our alliance: "For as long as it lasts." A frequently divorced friend at the table fell off his chair laughing.

> FRIEND
> I should have used that line at my last wedding.

Take your commitment seriously, but if it doesn't work don't take it personally. Ron and I wrote together for a year. We decided we each preferred writing alone. We are still good friends.

## Flutteration

When you fall in love with your partner, it will not be at the same time your partner falls in love with you. Ride it out. Falling in love is often a state of concentration. You become so focused on each other that there's an actual switch in the cortex of the brain, a kind of love brainwash. When the "flutteration" stops, the partnership will deepen. If you fall in love with each other at the same time, stop writing together. Get married.

## Partner as saboteur

Many partnerships that rise quickly and experience initial success, only to end just as quickly, are due to one partner acting as the saboteur. Watch out for partnerships that set you up for failure. You might sell a script very fast, so that the issue of the partnership is not how the two of you are going to get work, but how you are going to deal with instant success. If your partner can't handle it and drinks or gets sick, you will find yourself shoring him up and doing more than your part. This partnership and the job you've gotten will end just as abruptly as it began. You will say it was the partner's fault. Watch that when you choose someone you aren't choosing someone to fail for both of you. Have the strength of character to fail on your own.

*Inner Movie Axiom: Strong alliances occur best between two people who come together whole and through the partnership become even stronger.*

## The coward's guide to going it alone

Try the Buddy System.

Find another writer. Agree to each write a 21-Day Movie. It's sort of like going on a diet together. Brainstorm with one another. Use one another's support and suggestions. But each write his own movie.

# THE LOVED ONES' GUIDE
# TO THE CARE AND FEEDING OF
# A WOULD-BE SCREENWRITER

This section is assigned reading for anyone who loves you and is within shouting distance.

## When to give air and light

There will be a moment when your writer has left the planet. You can tell because there will be a hole in the air, a vacuum created by his or her leaving. If you try to reach in and pull them back, you will get your hand bitten. You will feel abandoned. You will do anything—interrupt, offer hot food on a tray at the typewriter. This is a mistake. They are gone. Trying to get them back from outer space (a) does not work and (b) will make you feel more abandoned. Know this: It isn't personal. Just because they've left the planet doesn't mean they don't love you. It means they are working, and if they are working, be patient. They will eventually finish working and be back and love you madly.

## When not to take protestations
  of love too seriously

They have written pages of genius. Their "lovability quotient" has gone up and they will want to dance with you while you're trying to cut vegetables. Put this outpouring of love in your pocket and lavish it on yourself tomorrow, when they are "worthless failures" and are incapable of sending or receiving any kind of love.

## Postponed gratification

If your writer is out to prove himself in his script, he might be inclined to this symptom: he can't love or be loved until the script is done. This is tough. He will not let you love him and yet he may be demanding of your love. Make a deal to have love and writing go on simultaneously. If you wait to love each other until after the script is done, the script will never get done and you'll never get on with life.

## Crisis intervention technique #1

If you are feeling unappreciated and aren't getting any cooperation from your writer whatsoever, open all the books you have in the house to the acknowledgement page. Notice the tone of indebtedness and apology all writers feel toward their loved ones—.

Be patient. You'll get yours.

## Happily ever after

I have a writer friend whose new wife was in terrible anguish. "He doesn't love me." We talked about it. She *was* willing to entertain the idea that he loved her, he was just writing. Rather than thinking of writing as the enemy, she embraced it and helped him every way she could. That made her feel part of, rather than apart from him. Seven years and two kids later he's a hotshot Hollywood writer and they have a great marriage. I went to their house for dinner. Jack was sound asleep in the hammock. Donna said, without missing a beat, "He's working on the second act."

## How to give Jekyll & Hyde equal time

As you know, this business of two people in love can be a real rollercoaster.

When you add writing to it, be aware that you don't use the writing as a focus for troubles that really belong to other realms of your relationship. *Inner Movie Axiom: Writing is not infidelity*.

When someone writes a script, especially a first script, it is usually a sincere attempt to better himself in some way. If that is a threatening concept to you, honor your writer by bettering yourself right along with him. Make a 21-day schedule of mutual activities of self-improvement. One day, let him recite his Oscar speech to inspire you off the couch and into aerobics. The next day, when he jumps down your throat, honor youself by not stuffing your face.

If you can dream individual dreams together, isn't that a lovely use of love?

## A word about believing

There is something very exciting about being in on someone's dream. When you can believe in the person and *want* their dream to come true, then you'll be fine and they will too.

# THE SCREENWRITER'S
# FAMILY PRIMER

Okay. We've spoken to your loved ones. They understand. They're with you on this thing. Now here's the same information for you.

Loved ones have uncanny radar. They will sense when your concentration has lifted you off the planet. They will know the exact moment. Even the dog will know. Especially the dog will know. And they will want you back. They will try all manner of subterfuge. Understand this: your creative powers are so mighty that those who live with you will experience an actual hole in the air where you once were. You've left a vacuum. Do not fight the loved ones. Do not ever fight the loved one. Embrace the fact that they want you back.

## How to grow into yourself

When you are growing, you are brand new. But there is a lag time here. Though you are brand new, your spouse and friends will be responding to you in the old way, at least until they see the new behavior and respond to that.

Have you ever seen a teenager throw a child-tantrum, shouting, "I want to be treated like an adult"?

The way to be treated like an adult is to act like an adult. So the way to be believed as a writer is to believe it yourself.

The way to change your loved ones' response to you is change *your behavior*. When you believe you are a writer; others will believe it too.

## The how-you-need-people multiple-choice love-life quiz

(a) Do you need people to believe in you and tell you that they do?

(b) Do you need to not tell anybody anything and go about your writing privately?

(c) Do you need for them to believe you are doing this, while at the same time you don't want to include them in your day-to-day feelings?

Your people are there to be anything you want them to be, you just have to ask them.

## Feast or famine

Remember the story of Chicken-Little, who pleaded, "Who will help me plant the corn?" Nobody would. But when the seed grew and the corn was harvested, everybody had time to eat it.

During the darkest, gloomiest day of Act II, when you think you can't go on, you'll call a friend and the friend will be no help whatsoever. Somehow you'll manage to pull yourself up by your bootstraps and finish your script.

The first one to come around will be this same friend, who will say, "I knew you could do it."

When you have no confidence and you need someone to talk you into yourself? Call a friend. Say this:

YOU
I have no confidence. Will you please
talk me into myself?

THE ENTIRE
WORLD POPULATION
(in unison)
We know you can do it!

## What to say to your spouse
### when you can't come to bed

Don't say anything. Give a huge, warm, long hug. Make rich, deep, meaningful love at your workspace, if that's where you are at the moment your spouse asks, "Are you coming to bed?" You may think you are sacrificing yourself for another. This is not true. Go ahead, 'Embrace' each other. Then, tuck your loved one in—happily. Now go to your work space. You're going to write *great* pages.

# WHY YOU'VE STOPPED;
# HOW TO KEEP GOING

There are four choices for writers who suffer over writing:

1 They can give up writing and suffer over that.
2 They can continue to write and suffer.
3 They can give up writing and not suffer.
4 They can continue to write and not suffer.

How do you want it? Choose now.
Okay, let's identify your blocks and solve them.

## Using your fear in your favor

Thomas Edison was afraid of the dark. Look what he did about it. He lit up the night.

You can use your creative energy to invent ways to stop or you can use the same energy to go forward and shed light on the darkness. Let's go.

## There are contradictions here

Some solutions will tell you to draw your attention to details, at other times you'll pull out to see the bigger picture. Success will be in your knowing when to take which action. As a general rule, if you are blocked it's because you are going one way (into or away from) and you need to turn and go in the opposite direction.

Are these some of your symptoms?

· You procrastinate.
· You wish you had more willpower.
· You wish you had a stronger, more positive attitude.
· You think you need a kick in the pants.
· You're lazy.

Great. Let's just get the big five out of the way immediately.

*Procrastination.* Procrastination is when you plan to do something and you don't do it.

*Inner Movie Axiom: The fault is not in that you didn't do it. The fault is in the thought that you would.*

Now change the word *procrastination* to *incubation* and let's move on.

*Willpower.* If you have willpower, raise your hand. Okay, keep it up there. Keep it up for ten minutes. Now drop it. What did you learn? You learned that you have a sore arm. Willpower often means doing something against your will.

*The Power of Negative Thinking.* Never deny what's going on. Always accept what's going on. Now you have the power to change it.

*Inner Movie Axiom: If you can accept it, you can transcend it.*

*A Kick in the Pants.* When you are asking for a kick in the pants, you really need a kiss on the cheek. Punishment, discipline comes from our mind outsmarting us; it reflects what we think we *should* be doing. But notice, instead, how easy it is to do what you *want* to do. When you were a kid you hated to get out of bed to go do your paper route but it was easy to get up at the crack of dawn for a fishing trip. *Inner Movie Axiom: We can do anything if we want to do it.* We think we need a kick in the pants to do what we don't want to do. Rather than using all that energy to get yourself to do what you don't want to do, do what you *do* want to do. Go fishing. Take along your typewriter.

Once you are ready, nothing can stop you. If you are not ready, no amount of kicks in the pants will get you to do it.

*Uses of Laziness.* On this page we could talk about how you never get started and you never follow through and you never finish, but aren't you tired of telling yourself that?

Let's go take a nap instead.

# NO SUCH THING
# AS WRITER'S BLOCK

If you don't believe there's no such thing as writer's block, sit down now. You can write ten pages titled "Why I am Blocked."

### Writer's block gets a bad rep

Every time you aren't writing, you blame "writer's block." You dump each incident into the black festering caldron of blockage, when maybe the real reason is that you'd rather go bowling.

If you're blocked because you'd rather go bowling, this requires a different treatment than if your block is fear of success because you will surpass your father. One of the main ways to unblock is to identify the block.

### We think we are so smart

Do you have this symptom: You think you have *it* inside and you are trying every which way to get *it* out and *it* refuses to come out. Let's say there's a big black box that is your creativity, and you think that what is inside the big black box is a little blonde puppy. But no matter what you do—shout, cajole, bribe—you can't get it to come out of the box. You know why? It's not a blonde puppy. *It* is not what you think it is, and your preconception of what it is *keeps it in there*.

So do this: (1) Relinquish the mistaken idea that it's a puppy. (2) *Agree* that there is something in the box, and it would like to come out. (3) *Let* it out. (4) Now that you've *let* it out, you can see what it really is.

How can you name what you've created before you create it? Let it out. See what it is. Maybe it *is* a puppy, but with twelve feet and green spots. Whatever it is that wants to come out, it's much greater than you think. And you're thinking you know what it is, keeps it in there and keeps it common.

## Releasing yourself from the tyranny of brilliant writing

I think I know why Shakespeare could write so well—he didn't have to compare himself to Shakespeare!

Do you think your writing has to be Shakespearean in tone and lofty in lugubrious profundity? All you have to do as a writer is run up to your reader and say, "Hey, I gotta tell you this stuff."

## This is the worst feeling in the world

If writing is painful, don't blame writing, blame pain. It's not writing's fault, because when you are writing and it is flowing, it's one of the best feelings you'll ever experience. Writing doesn't hurt; stopping hurts. If you are in a morass of the worst feelings in the world because you can't write, sit down now. Write about it. Take comfort in the sanctuary of writing before choosing to go back to stoppage.

## Advantages of writer's block

Except for the obligatory paraphernalia that declares you are a writer, a writer's block is the only evidence you have that you are a writer. Do this: go buy a pipe; sew suede elbow patches on your tweed sportscoat. Or best of all, fill pages. You think because you don't have pages you are not a writer. So fill pages. An eight-minute short story on your dog, a twelve-page list of all the people you ever knew, know now, and, will know in your lifetime. Fill pages, let them tell you that you are a writer. (PS: If you want to be a doctor, you first *become* a doctor, with training and time. If you want to be a writer, let yourself *become* a writer.)

## Where am I
## and why does it hurt so bad?

*Inner Movie Axiom: Signs of struggle are symptoms. They are there to show you to go another way.*

Notice when you are struggling. You feel lousy. That's enough. Just stay with how you feel. You will find yourself trying to get out of the feeling. *That's* struggle.

You will think, "What's the matter with me? Why do I feel so bad? I'm stupid."

You will go from analyzing to criticizing, until your thinking part talks your feeling part into feeling much worse.

That's why it's called struggle, because you're not accepting how you feel. The act of not accepting the feeling is struggle.

So when you are in a funk, stay with the feeling. Don't add more pressure on yourself to get out of the feeling.

When you find your mind snooping around your feelings, it's your mind's duty to leave yourself alone.

Here's the job you can give your mind to do:

*You* stay with the feelings, let *your mind* notice your behavior. Your behavior will give you information about why you're feeling awful.

Here's one way to do that . . . .

## Talking yourself into yourself

First notice what you say when you're talking to yourself:

"I'm no good."

"I can't do this."

Would you let anybody talk to you like that? You'd probably sue. Now turn those statements around:

"I am unlimited."

"I can do what I want."

Write a fan letter to yourself now. Go ahead, write for eight minutes.

## How to stop giving yourself
### rejection slips

The way to stop rejection is to accept it. Accept rejection. That's the way it is. Rejection is not personal. Don't make it personal.

I spoke to a man who sailed around the world alone. He was interested in conquering the sea. Somewhere off the coast of South America his boat capsized and he spent forty days floating on a piece of wreckage contemplating the sea he set out to conquer. It was then he understood two things: (1) he would not conquer the sea, and (2) the sea was not out to conquer him. It was not going to win while he lost. He learned that the sea is indifferent.

When we face rejection we would rather cultivate a relationship of rage over who rejects us than accept that they are indifferent.

Accept it. Don't drown yourself.

## How to tell when your mind wants recess

Do you have these symptoms? Do you have ants in your pants? Are you full of the dickens, suffering from acute sassiness? Remedy: Go play.

We don't want you to have to use all your energy just to keep yourself in the chair. Then there's no energy left for you to do the work. So go. Get it out of your system. See you later.

## 100 ways to lighten up

Go out into nature. Nature is smarter than we are. It will reset your pace, untangle the knots you've gotten yourself into. Watch a bird. Have a meaningful conversation with an oak tree.

Go to the park. Slide down the slide. Leave your anguish at the top. Slide away from it.

Fly a kite, write your unclear problems across its face. See it way up there and get a new perspective.

Invite yourself to a friend's house to be taken care of for the weekend.

Take care of someone else's problems.

Tell yourself a terrible joke in the mirror.

Stand on your head.

Go to the store. Smell all the soaps. Pick out the perfect one. Buy a candle too. Go home. Take a long, hot candlelit bath or shower. Fall asleep.

Finish this list.

Notice, the way to start writing has nothing to do with writing.

# ADVANCED HYPOCHONDRIA,
# A CHRONIC APPROACH

**How to distinguish between
the heebie-jeebies and a bump in the script**

All right, I'm going to be indelicate here. This is a bathroom story. If you don't want to hear about it, turn the page.

The assignment was my first hour-long film show. "Rush job" (It's always a rush job). "Do it in four days." Four days! I got the trots. My entire career and a mega-figure deal were riding on this. I was overwhelmed. So I did what every healthy writer does. I got symptoms, death symptoms. Actually they were symptoms of life, and *I knew it*. I tried to talk myself out of it—no dice. So I went to a doctor who gave me a big pill to take and told me to go to bed. Terrific, permission to sleep. I went home, sat on the bed, looked at the pill. What was this thing? It was the size of an elephant tranquilizer. I knew that if I took it I'd be out for the four days I needed to get the script written. There comes a moment in everyone's life—you can zig or you can zag, and I swear the rest of your life depends on it. I got up slowly and went to the typewriter, set it up in the bathroom, and typed this contract to myself. "Hello, Body, this is Free Will talking. You can be sick all you want. . . . I'm in this bathroom to accommodate you. But here's what: I'm going to write this script with you or without you. Love, Viki." An hour later I was well into Act I and well out of the bathroom, feeling fine.

## Hypochondria

Writers are among the world's more clever hypochondriacs. As eccentric as your symptoms are, another screenwriter has had them before you and lived. Touch just between your breastbone, there's a kind of lumpy mass. This is your sternum. Everyone has one, even nonwriters. You might not have noticed it until now. Often would-be writers discover this as they roll a blank sheet of paper into the typewriter. You are not going to die of this. Look for something else.

You will tend to pick out vague symptoms that come and go. Something nerverelated, or an itch. Something that requires research. An itch usually means the story's ready to come out, but you're not ready to let it out.

## Symptoms of being a writer

*Pulled muscle*. You're trying too hard to force it.

*Throwing up*. Catharsis. It's all coming up. The next day after this is usually a great writing day.

*No energy*. There's a lot of work you're doing on the inside, but you have nothing to show on paper, so you think you're a failure. You aren't. The thinking that you're a failure is what is keeping the block, and that's what's taking your energy. It will come out when it's ready, usually when you start to itch.

*Blurred vision*. You don't want to look at the truth that's coming out of your script. It's all coming at you too fast. You might even find yourself wincing. You will furrow your brow. Practice looking at something—a coffee cup—for a long time with no judgment. Notice what there is to see about it. Get used to the idea that seeing something doesn't mean it's going to get you.

Here's another blurred vision reducer, look to the horizon. Give your eye a distant vision. See the big picture, disengage from a squint-eyed view of the details.

*Shortness of breath*. One student called me in the night. He was sure he had forgotten how to breathe. He agreed to jog around the kitchen table. Within minutes he was breathing so hard even he could hear it. Shortness of breath often occurs when you get a glimpse of what you're in for, and it scares you. It indicates that you're worried about being out of control.

*Backache.* As in "get off my back." This is usually a sign of pressure. You might be worried that you'll go backwards. Or it might mean you want to back off and lie down in life and not do anything. Give yourself time to just loll around. Backache, more than any other symptom, is a sign of career change. When you know you have to get out of one way of life and you don't know what you're moving toward, backache provides permission to lie down and think. Do an eight-minute ache escape instead. Lie down, let the noise inside you tell you what it wants. Listen and take action. Take care of your life.

These are just a few symptoms. I'm sure you'll think of your own.

## Why you get the flu on page 90

This is a symptom of resisting progress. The person you are when you finish is going to be a little different than the person you were when you began. You need a moment to stand at the doorway and look back at the place you're leaving before you walk through the door. This is a good use of flu. It gives you a few days to stop. Rest up, when you're ready you'll move very fast.

## One unauthorized, nonmedical explanation of hypochondria

When you finally commit to writing and quit your day job, you will go from being outer directed—up by alarm clock, reacting to co-workers, staving off hunger until your lunch hour—to being inner directed. All decisions are yours, it's quiet, you can hear your heartbeat. You are getting acquainted with the stranger in your body. Like a new house when you move into it, there are all those funny noises. You will think of all this new stuff as symptoms.

*Inner Movie Axiom: Let your body work for you. Don't work against your body.*

# STAGES
# AND PHASES

When you fill blank pages, you're in the business of going from *nothing* to *beingness*. Think of making a baby. There is action, conception, gestation, reaction, adjustment to reaction, event. Bringing a thing into existence, whether it's a baby or a script, has many *stages and phases*. You may want to ask, "what's wrong with me?" But there's nothing wrong with you—it's the nature of bringing a thing into existence.

## Decision making 101

If you have a decision to make, do you

- weigh the facts,
- examine how you feel about it,
- determine what you want,
- and then make the decision?

Fine, but then what?

Now you have to *take an action*. If you don't take an action, you will go back and make the same decision over again.

*Inner Movie Axiom: Always starting at the beginning keeps you at the beginning.*

## If you're scared to move on

Scared is a feeling. Honor it. If you ignore it, you'll move from decision to confusion. Since you already made a decision, take the action. Action is something to do. Then you have to react to the action, and so forth. If what scares you about moving on is that you're not ready, then the action to take is—get ready.

Seek information, ask questions.

Look for potential solutions, then enact them. Take them one by one and try them out. The only mistake is to stay stuck. Move.

## Think less, do more

Consolidate the time between thought and action. Just take action.

## When the plot thickens

There will come a moment when you look and you see that the thing got bigger and deeper and broader and awesome. You will be overwhelmed. It's *too* much, the story's *too* big. The feelings are *too* real. Good, now you're onto something. This is a moment at which you will want to stop and put it in the closet. Go ahead, put it away if you must, but it will send out vapors every time you walk past it. So—take it out. Give it a new outfit. Change notebooks. Acquaint yourself with it in a new way.

It's taken on a life of its own. It's starting to breathe whether you like it or not.

## The 1000-page shuffle/how to divide and conquer

I have a client who came in the door overwrought, overwhelmed, overbudget. She had a pile of papers in a totebag. This is a sign. She read through some, and I noticed that as she read, she'd turn one paper face down, and then the next she'd put behind the pile. She had no organization, no rhythm, no reason. We did something revolutionary. We numbered the pages.

Often when you have a thousand pages it's because your script is written twelve different ways. Make decisions. This version or that one. No more writing; you've already got it. Go with what you have.

Stand behind it. Otherwise you get more and more material that isn't quite right. Take a stand and make one strong statement.

# WHAT HAPPENS
# WHEN I GET STUCK?

You may think that in order to start you have to (a) know what to do and (b) have confidence you'll do it. This is not true.

*Inner Movie Axiom: "You don't have to know what you're doing to do it."*

One of the reasons we prepare for something beforehand is so we can feel confident about jumping feet first into the abyss. But this doesn't work, because confidence is a feeling we acquire *after* trying a task and succeeding at it. It is not a quality we can have *before* we try the task.

Just because you lack *confidence* doesn't mean you lack *competence*. If you don't know what you're doing—do it. It's the best way to find out *how to do it*.

## This is not a test

*Inner Movie Axiom: There are no tests*. You are not here to be tested unless you choose to test yourself.

Okay, you want to do this test, but notice where you can give yourself permission to not make it so hard.

You might feel that you have to write a script to "prove" yourself. Proving yourself is a job you give yourself for however long and arduous a time you determine, at the end of which you can stop and declare yourself as having passed the test that nobody asked you to take.

*Inner Movie Axiom: You don't prove nothing 'til you have nothing to prove.*

## A through Z = B

Here's what we do. We build mountains and then we climb them. We could just as well have walked across the street. See where you can give yourself a shorter journey.

## If it's impossible, don't do it

If you feel as if you can't go on—don't.

Are you having the worst possible time and nothing is working?

No one asked for this script of yours, and chances are no one's going to notice if you don't finish it. *You* decided to do this. You could have just as arbitrarily decided to be a jackhammer operator. Is it important for you to "be somebody"? Is that why you want to do this? Look at how you're feeling—like somebody? No, you're feeling like nobody. Ask yourself some hard questions: Did you choose this task to fail at it? If you have, guess what—you succeeded. You achieved your goal. Now lighten up and let people like you *as is*—you're somebody right now.

*Inner Movie Axiom: Definition of a winner—If the goal doesn't work, change it and win.*

## Permission to stop

This is just a movie. It is *not* you. You will live whether or not you finish the script. You just think you won't. You're holding on too tight; you have yourself invested here.

Make a decision now. Can you go on with the script? Can you find the way to move forward? If you can't, then let it go. Letting it go is also forward movement.

If you don't want to do something, then acknowledge that you don't want to. Don't pretend to try. Use that energy to do what you *do* want to do.

# YOUR DREAM

### The reality about fantasy

I have an old friend I sometimes invite to screenings. She has a fantasy of being a writer: "I could write that, if I weren't in the secretarial pool." I always know where to find her the next day. She's in the secretarial pool.

Some fantasies are fantasies, you don't want them to come true. It's okay. Just know that.

### Jealousy

*Inner Movie Axiom: You are not someone else.*

I get calls all the time from clients who say they just came from a movie that was terrible. How did that "dreck" get produced, when their movie is in the drawer and it's a hundred times better?

One client came in last week with a cover of *People* magazine. "Why is she on this cover? I have more talent in my big toe than she has in her whole body."

There's the problem. When was the last time you saw a cover picture of a big toe?

Less is more. *Inner Movie Axiom: You have a million ideas. You don't need that many.* Look at who makes you jealous. Someone who doesn't have one fifth of your talent. Find out what she does have that you don't have. Let who you are jealous of teach you something.

## How a dream comes true

You need to believe in your dream.

If you're having trouble getting your dream to come true, then your dream isn't big enough. Do you want a beach house or a Maserati?

Is that all?

Let's fine tune your dream now.

Why do you want a beach house? "To show them"? "To feel like somebody"? "To get girls"? Find what you really want. Dreams are usually for more life.

One of my students, Lucy, wanted to be on the cover of *People* magazine. We did this exercise: "So that . . . ."

Write your dream at the top of the page. Now go back, back, back to its source using "So that." For example: "I want to be in *People* magazine *so that* people will see me. *So that* I'm admired. *So that* Aunt Rose will see a copy in the supermarket and call my mom. *So that* my mom will get calls from everybody in the neighborhood. *So that* she will be proud of me."

Once you find the source of your desire for fame or wealth, you are free to go directly to that need and fill it. Because here's the secret of success: If you fill the need *first*, then you will succeed; if you try to succeed to fill the need, you can only succeed in spite of it.

## The difference between a dream and a goal

A dream is an all-powerful, intense wish for yourself. It's your heart talking.

A goal is how your head plans to realize it.

I had two friends who bought their mega-buck dream estates at about the same time. One conferred with his financial counselors and made a long-term plan to keep the house even if his humongous income suddenly dried up. The other bought his dream house on the spur of the moment. You might say a very expensive impulse buy.

The first is still living in and loving his house. The second lived in his for eight months, with no furniture, until the whole dream became a nightmare.

Do you want your dream to become a nightmare or do you want your dream to come true?

If you want to make your dream come true, change it to a reality. That's what coming true means—no longer a dream.

## When is someday?

Go directly to your dream. If you think you have to go to graduate school first, or write TV before you write films, or retire to have time—you don't. *Inner Movie Axiom: Go directly to your dream.*

## No-fault living

Do you think success goes to the lucky, to the other guy who doesn't have your problems?

Success goes to the one who has as many problems, but solves them.

You have problems so that you can do with them what you choose. You can deny them, avoid them, become embroiled in them, or solve them and move on.

# ACTION

## Just do the damn thing

Dustin Hoffman's method of acting is to draw the character out from inside himself.

Laurence Olivier's method is to wear the character as a mask.

Each actor respects the other enormously.

They were filming *Marathon Man* together when Dustin had some difficulty with his part.

Olivier said, "Why don't you try acting, dear boy?"

Are you getting out of your way so you can have more things be in your way? Know when the shortest distance is directly to the finish line. Do it!

## A final word on the inner enemy

Any blocks you have can be reduced to one cause: You don't think enough of yourself.

Go to a mirror, say "I love you." Mean it. You'll be fine.

The
Last Word

# THERE'S NO BUSINESS
# LIKE SHOW BUSINESS

The you who started the script is different from the you who finishes it. That new you is the one who will sell it.

*Inner Movie Axiom: If you try to sell it before you write it, you won't accomplish either.*

### Paranoia

Everyone thinks his idea is unique; that his script is special, and that everyone else is out to steal it. This is true. Your script *is* special; your idea *is* unique. It will be stolen. Not because anybody will see it; but because it will just come out of another typewriter across the state. This phenomenon reflects the workings of "collective unconscious," and it happens all the time.

(If it makes you feel better, send a copy of your script to yourself by registered mail. Or register it at the Writers Guild of America, 8955 Beverly Boulevard, Los Angeles, California, 90048; for a nominal fee you can register your completed script and get a registration number. This gives you proof of when you came up with the idea.)

### How do I get an agent?

Any way you can.

Here is where the real creativity comes in. Send it to his

mother. Have your third cousin who used to be a caddy for Jerry Vale get you a personal reference. Also, you might want to write to the Writers Guild again. For a nominal fee, they will send you a list of accredited agents. Get the list. Send your material. You will get it back unopened. It will break your heart. Send it out again.

## Do I need an agent?

An agent will not get you work. (Ask anybody who has one.) What you are after is a partnership. You supply terrific material; he will hustle meetings. You get terrific response at meetings; he draws up the contracts. Agent or not, go everywhere, see everyone. But don't even bother until you have a well-written script.

When you send your script to a studio they will require that you sign a release form before they look at it. This is standard procedure. Do not be over-anxious about what you might be signing away. You are in the business now. Work with the realities of how the business is done.

## What do I do until I get an agent?

Think of everyone you know who might help get your script sold or produced. Decide what actor you want to play the lead and send it to him.

You might want to find backers who will invest in your movie. Hollywood is not the only place to look.

Meanwhile, continue to send it to agents, as you continue to send it to producers, directors, actors, backers.

Of course, write another script. If you are out to sell yourself as a writer, let's see a body of work.

## Can I succeed in Hollywood if I live in Buffalo?

Well, there's always postage stamps.

Besides, I noticed something when I was working in situation comedy. The writers from outside of Hollywood were not jaded. They could look at a show on the air and see just the show and not the goobleygook that might be behind it. This gave them a potentially clearer vision. You have the opportunity to come up with the one fresh idea that Hollywood hasn't thought of.

If you do decide to move to Hollywood—Warning: Fame and fortune will take a while so go ahead, unpack the U-Haul.

## How to know when you're in the business

What do you want? Do you want to just sell your 21-Day movie for megabucks and still keep your job at the turnpike tollbooth? Then go to a big producer and rely on your blockbuster story to catapult itself onto the screen.

If you want to be a writer in Hollywood and earn your living as a writer, then you are selling *you*, not the script. Use the script to get yourself invited, to meet everybody, to "get acquainted" and pitch other stories. If you do this long enough, you will eventually build a career.

This is just a quick list of suggestions as to how to sell your script. There's of course more to it than we've talked about here. But here's the single most effective way to have your script become a movie:

Write it the best way you can.

Dear One,

Thank you for letting me be a part of your Inner Movie. Whether you decide to put your script in the drawer or get it on the screen, I hope that the richness of the experience has been infinite for you. (If infinite richness isn't enough then I also wish you fame and fortune. Once you get your heart set on something you might as well have it.)

If you would like news of tapes and seminars, write to me. Include one dollar to help defray mailing costs. (Please do not send scripts.) I'll let you know when I'll be in your town giving a talk. And of course, I'll see you through my next book. This isn't the end, "this is the beginning of a beautiful friendship."

Your fellow writer,

Viki King

P.O. Box 563
Malibu, California
90265

# ORDER FORM

THE INNER MOVIE METHOD
Cassette Tapes

THE 9-MINUTE MOVIE
What Goes on Pages 1, 3, 10, 30, 45, 60, 75, 90, 120

NO MORE WRITER'S BLOCK
How to Embrace The Impossible Obstacles

WHAT'S THE STORY
How To Know What You Want To Say.And Say It

| Qty. | Item | Price | Total |
|------|------|-------|-------|
| ____ | THE 9-MINUTE MOVIE | $9.95 | _____ |
| ____ | NO MORE WRITER'S BLOCK | $9.95 | _____ |
| ____ | WHAT'S THE STORY | $9.95 | _____ |
| | | SUBTOTAL | _____ |
| | add $1.40 per tape shipping and handling | | _____ |
| | Calif. residents add 6.5% sales tax | | _____ |
| | | TOTAL | _____ |

NAME: _____

ADDRESS: _____

CITY, STATE, ZIP: _____

*send check or money order to:*

   Viki King
   P.O. Box 563
   Malibu, California 90265

*Handling charges and prices subject to change without notice.*

# INDEX